Additional Praise for
Rediscovery of Awe

"*Rediscovery of Awe* is amazingly revolutionary!"
> —Natalie Rogers, Ph.D., author of *The Creative Connection:*
> *Expressive Arts as Healing*

"In a welcome awakening of the finest wisdom of Humanistic Psychology, Kirk Schneider leads us to rediscover a long-forgotten sense of awe in the very center of our lives."
> —Allan Combs; author of *The Radiance of Being:*
> *Understanding the Grand Integral Vision*

"Awe is the stone rejected by many parts of Western civilization with its materialist and reductionist assumptions, but this book makes awe a cornerstone of a new and intriguing theory about human life."
> —David Elkins, Ph.D., Author of *Beyond Religion,*
> Professor of Psychology Emeritus, Pepperdine University

"Really excellent... Reading *Rediscovery of Awe* was like wrestling with holy writ."
> —E. Mark Stern, Ed.D., Professor of Psychology Emeritus, Iona College,
> Editor Emeritus, *The Psychotherapy Patient.* former president of
> Division 36 (Psychology of Religion) of the APA

"Kirk Schneider maintains that the awesomeness of life has been ignored by most psychologists and psychotherapists, but he brings it front and center. His prescription for 'awe-based living' draws upon developmental studies, social criticism, existential philosophy, literary and cinematic classics, and his own case studies. The result is a book that throws its net widely, drawing together faith, magnificence, mystery, the spirit of Carnival, and other elements needed for a juicy stew. *Rediscovery of Awe* presents a challenging recipe, and its readers will savor every chapter of this provocative volume."
> —Stanley Krippner, Ph.D., Co-editor, *Varieties of Anomalous Experience*
> and recipient of the APA award, '2002 Distinguished Contribution
> to the International Advancement of Psychology'

REDISCOVERY OF AWE

SPLENDOR, MYSTERY, AND THE FLUID CENTER OF LIFE

Kirk J. Schneider, Ph.D.

Paragon House
St. Paul, Minnesota

Published in the United States by

Paragon House
2285 University Avenue West
St. Paul, Minnesota 55114

Copyright © 2004 by Paragon House

Earlier versions of parts of this book appeared in the following publications:
"Hitchcock's *Vertigo*: An existential view of spirituality." *The Journal of Humanistic Psychology*, Vol. 33, Spring, 1993, 91–100.
"The fluid center: A third millennium challenge to culture." *The Humanistic Psychologist*, Vol. 27, Spring, 1999, 114–130.
"Standing in awe: The cosmic dimensions of effective psychotherapy." *The Psychotherapy Patient*, Vol. 11, No. 3/4, 2001, 123–127.
"The fluid center: An awe-based challenge to humanity." *The Journal of Humanistic Psychology*, Vol. 43, No. 3, 2003, 133–145.
"Existential-humanistic psychotherapies." In A. Gurman and S. Messer, eds., *Essential psychotherapies* (New York: Guilford Press, 2003), 149–181.
"Enchanted Agnosticism." *Tikkun*, Vol. 18, July/August, 2003, 41–43.

Library of Congress Catalog-in-Publication Data

Schneider, Kirk J.
  Rediscovery of awe : splendor, mystery, and the fluid center of life /
Kirk J. Schneider.-- 1st ed.
    p. cm.
  Includes bibliographical references.
  ISBN 1-55778-834-0 (pbk. : alk. paper)
  1. Awe. 2. Humanistic psychology. I. Title.

  BF575.A9S36 2004
  150.19'86--dc22

                           2004000378

Manufactured in the United States of America

The paper used in this publication meets the minimum requirements of American National Standard for Information Sciences—Permanence of Paper for Printed Library Materials, ANSIZ39.48-1984.

10 9 8 7 6 5 4 3 2 1

For current information about all releases from Paragon House,
visit the web site at http://www.paragonhouse.com

To my clients, who have taught me much.
And to my son, Benjamin, who has taught me most.

Contents

Part III: The Fluid Center of Faith

Acknowledgments

This book began as an invited address to the Department of Psychology of Duquesne University in 1996. Following the events of September 11, 2001, I became mobilized to expand the aforementioned into a treatise. Because treatises of this sort (which provide neither simple answers nor pat formulas) are rather disparaged in these expedience-minded times, my deepest appreciation goes to those unwavering souls who stuck by me and lent tangible, "hands-on" support. Among these stalwarts were: Ed Mendelowitz, Ilene Serlin, Michael Cooper, John Galvin, Dennis Portnoy, Donald Cooper, Corbett Williams, Gerardo Pacheco, Alan Combs, Daniel Helminiak, David Elkins, Daniel Burston, Maurice Friedman, Peggy Salkind, David Wulff, Tom Greening, Richard Wiseman, Irena Raulinaitis, Laura and Alvin Siegal, and my loving wife, Jurate. To those whom I have inadvertently overlooked, my sincere apologies; please know that I am grateful to you.

I would also like to extend a special thanks to Jeffrey Alan Bricker and E. Mark Stern who provided early, critical feedback that was pivotal to the manuscript's evolution.

Further, I would like to thank Gordon Anderson, Rosemary Yokoi, and Paragon House for their willingness to risk where others dared not venture.

Finally, I would like to acknowledge Ernest Becker, whose lifetime (and deathbed) candor ever rekindles my awe.

Foreword

At the center of this book lies a powerful metaphor: the "fluid center." Indeed, by combining "fluid" and "center" Schneider breaks new ground. Our general tendency is to imagine the center of things as solid or at the very least structured. "Fluid center," in contrast, evokes a sense of deep significance at the heart of things without any rigid forms or lines. Schneider defines "fluid center," in fact, as "structured inclusiveness—the richest possible range of experience within the most suitable parameters of support." An excellent example of this is his description of "awe-based psychotherapy," which is "both systematic and flexible; practical yet daring."

The title of Schneider's book is *Rediscovery of Awe*, and that is precisely what this book is. Here, too, we are stretched to the limit by a paradox far outside our ordinary expectations. Even humanist and existentialist psychologists are still wedded to science or to concrete phenomena and not to something as insubstantial as "awe." Awe lies at the center of my great friend Abraham Joshua Heschel's philosophy of religion. But we do not expect it to be the touchstone of reality of even such an outstanding existentialist psychologist as Kirk Schneider.

When we turn to the contents of the book itself, we find a range and scope far beyond that of any living psychologist that I know, and I know most of the outstanding ones. If we imagine that Schneider's focus will be mostly on religion, theology, mysticism, or the transcendent, we shall be astonished to find that much of his book deals with education and social problems, including quite specific and concrete suggestions for both fields.

It may seem strange to some that Schneider, who has often published criticisms of transpersonal psychology, as it is adumbrated by Kenneth Wilber and others, is nonetheless open to the transcendent in a way that few psychologists are. "The fluid center," as Schneider writes in the introduction to his book, "begins and unfolds through awe, the humility and wonder of living. It is precisely through awe that we come to know how daunting life is and how readily our presumptions crumble, and yet, conversely, it is precisely through awe that we are awakened to life's majesty."

Schneider's book is a remarkable synthesis of all his past published work, such as his book on horror and the holy, plus new central themes such as the spirit of carnival, depth therapy as social vision, and responsibility as the corollary of magnificence and mystery. Schneider's personal synthesis is at the same time an address and challenge not only to every psychologist but also to every thoughtful person in the field of helping, healing, education, and social betterment. It is impossible to overestimate its significance.

—Maurice Friedman, Ph.D., Professor Emeritus
San Diego State University

Background

Awe is the finest portion of mankind:
However scarce the world may make this sense—
In awe one feels profoundly the immense.

—Johann von Goethe (*Faust*, Part II)[1]

The awesomeness of life is the starting point for psychology. Any psychology worth its name must begin with this premise.

By awesomeness, I mean first of all, mystery—incomprehensibility, and second of all, magnificence—bedazzlement. I am not simply speaking here of the sentiment we experience when we gaze at stars (or athletes, or, God forbid, U.S. military campaigns!); I am speaking of the brute awareness that we exist at all.

Awe is not a very comfortable standpoint for many people. (Academic psychology, for example, has virtually ignored it).[2] Hence, all about us today, we see avoidance of awe—by burying ourselves in materialist science, for example, or in absolutist religious positions; or by locking ourselves into systems, whether corporate, familial, or consumerist; or by stupefying ourselves with drugs. We also, ironically, see the avoidance of awe in positions that profess to embrace life's multiplicity. Some postmodernists, for example, imply that awe is a historical or cultural artifact, as profound or significant as any other historical or cultural perspective.[3]

More than ever before, it seems to me, we are in need of the wisdom that awe inspires. We are in need of paradoxical wisdom. We need to see the complexity of things, the wholeness of things, which means the incompleteness and simplicity of things at the same time. We need to see that as soon as we polarize, we partialize our understanding. As soon as we fixate, even if we fixate on what appears to be open and multiple, we lose the vitality of our being, the elasticity of our being, and the poignant predicament of our being.

While our fixating and partializing may be less blatant today than they were in the past, they are no less menacing. The forms have changed, but the tendencies have not quieted. Whereas feudal lords and kings may have once dominated the landscape, now it is advertising and mass production—the quicker, the slicker, the better. Whereas religious codes once reigned, we now have computer, marketing, and media codes. Of course, (fundamentalist) backlashes are beginning to cluster about us as well. Sometimes these backlashes are violent and sometimes they are subtle, but one point strikes clear: We are just as threatened by regressions to the premodern as we are by transgressions of the modern and postmodern. Benjamin Barber's notion of Jihad vs. McWorld—a nightmare dominated by popes, mullahs, and rabbis on the one hand, and CEOs, brokers, and technowizards on the other—may not be that far off.[4]

In this book, I will examine the variety of ways that people neglect awe, as above; but primarily, and most importantly, I will focus on a trend that is poised to rival the former. This is a trend or consciousness that has many distinguished roots: the Old and New Testaments, Gnostic writings, spiritual and mystical traditions, and most recently, romantic and existential positions. But it is also a consciousness that has yet to be fully formed. This book, then, represents my own modest attempt to elaborate this consciousness—an awe-based perspective that I call the "fluid center."

Introduction

The starting point of consciousness is awe. I think that is pretty well established. The starting point for most religions, philosophies, and spiritual beliefs is also that mixture of "dread, veneration, and wonder" termed awe. This, too, is well established.[1] That contemporary psychology virtually ignores these facts in favor of some odd form of materialism is a wonder in itself![2]

In beginning with awe, certain points become immediately evident. The first point is that we as human beings experience the world (cosmos, being) as overwhelming. From the moment we are aware, we become aware of our meagerness. From the moment we reflect on ourselves and the world, we sense how hopeless, helpless, and vulnerable we are. And yet, close on the heels of this shuddering despair of ours is a riveting sense of possibility about our lot. As much as we are apart from that which surrounds us, we are also a part of it, partners to it. We are thrilled, enthralled, and exalted by our condition as much as it perplexes and overpowers us. If life is an open sea within which we may drown, then it is also a yielding sea within which we may meld and merge.

Yet life and experience teach us that if we lean too heavily toward one or the other aspect of our awe, we get into trouble. If we ally ourselves with our meagerness, for example, we court cynicism and despair. Conversely, if we rely too strongly on our greatness, we solicit hubris and self-destruction. Why is it then that, despite the clarity of these scenarios, so many of us in so many walks of life lapse into one or the other pole that fosters so much grief? My reply is that to fully accept awe in our lives is to fully accept the paradox, ambiguity, and absurdity of our condition. It is to fully accept that no matter what we think, feel, or do, it is always both wondrous and inept. It is wondrous because we can think, feel, or do at all, that something beyond us *enables* us to think, feel, or do; and it is inept because it is inevitably partial. We are as loath to admit our wormlikeness when we feel godlike, as we are terrified to accept our godlikeness when we feel wormlike.

An alternative to denying the craziness of our condition, which only leads to greater craziness, is to *live* the craziness of our condition, which leads to a kind of quirky vitality, a "crazy wisdom."[3] But to live in our craziness, our awe, is an exceedingly challenging task—and it becomes even more challenging when we extrapolate the idea to groups, cultures, and, eventually, the world. The first element in this challenge is to embrace both doubt and faith—humility and boldness—simultaneously. It is a capacity to be radically uncertain and yet risk commitment despite that uncertainty. Further, it is a capacity to bracket thoughts, feelings, and actions while at the same time affirming them; a capacity to see the potential for revision of a cause or project while at the same time being impassioned about them; and a capacity to engage individual thoughts, feelings, and actions while at the same time being mindful of their collective implications.

Few people are able to tolerate such paradoxical qualities and yet more seem to be recognizing their value. Growing numbers of people seem to recognize that fixation upon our possibilities is as debilitating as obsession with our impotencies, and that the rejuvenating answer lies somewhere in between. One of the freshest examples of this realization is the upheaval of 1960s America. Whereas the 50s were characterized by the constricting Victorian and Puritan values of earlier eras, the 60s were marked by extreme opposition to those values. If closed sexual and moral lifestyles were the bane of earlier American life, then chaotic sexual and moral lifestyles of the 60s were its destructive equivalent. The rejuvenating alternative, however, is some unprecedented amalgam of qualities: structure, depth, and discipline, but also elasticity, breadth, and spontaneity. There needs to be a humility before existence, but also a defiance and engagement as well.

Yet the rejuvenating alternative is not at all a "solution" in the classic sense; it is simply a vision that I have found promising. The term I have come to employ for this topsy-turvy vision is the "fluid center." Fluidity refers to our capacity (and need) to be expansive—flexible, versatile—when called for, and centeredness refers to our capacity (and need) to be constrained—where appropriate. Taken together, fluidity and centeredness acknowledge the controlled mayhem of so many of our lives, and indeed, of existence itself.

The great question of course is how we fruitfully combine fluidity and centeredness so as to revitalize individual and collective lives. After all, one may ask, are not many of the principles of civilization based on both firmness and flexibility, the "happy medium," or the "golden mean?" Is not the American Constitution, as well as much of the Western world's economic and social policies, based on checks and balances? Does not much of psychology teach moderation, the reconciling of conflicting forces, either within individuals or among individuals? To these questions, I answer both yes and no. Yes, much of civilization is based on the provision of "reasonable" degrees of freedom within orderly rules and principles; and yes, conventional psychology concerns itself with moderation and the like. But at the same time, there are many problems with these conventional maxims of balance. First, many people do not adhere to them—I refer here to the rampant problems with addictions, overeating, and overspending in our society, not to mention despair, bigotry, and violence. Second, even when people do adhere to conventional notions of balance and moderation in our society, they often do not find them very satisfying; if it were otherwise, then there would be much less gravitation to the extremes referred to above. The conventional center, then, is a rather dull and static one for many, and not at all what I have in mind with my notion of "fluidity" within centeredness. What, then, do I have in mind, and how are we to cultivate it in this atrophied world? We will explore these questions over a broad range of psychospiritual domains—from child raising to education, and from work to religion and ethics—but first, some background is in order.

PART I:

What Has Been Lost and How It
Can Be Recovered

1

The Quest for a Comprehensive Psychology

If you are going to have a myth of New Being, then like
Tillich, you have to use this myth as a call to the highest and most difficult effort—and not to simple joy. A
creative myth is not simply a relapse into comfortable
illusion; it has to be as bold as possible in order to be
truly generative.

—Ernest Becker (*Denial of death*, 1973, p. 278)

The quest for a comprehensive psychology, a psychology of profundity, with as few consolations about the human condition as
possible, has been the province of but a few bold inquirers. Generally, such quests are relegated to the margins of history, have few
organized adherents, and find little support among conventional
scholars. There is, however, an identifiable strain of scholarship
that stretches far back into the history of ideas, and that might
be called a science of humanity (or psychological anthropology),
that is pertinent to our purposes in this book. Momentarily, we
will look closer at this lineage, but before we do, let us consider the
views from which it departs. In this way, we can better understand
what the science of humanity affirms.

There are three basic traps, to which most human science
paradigms succumb—behavioral reductionism, spiritual puritanism, and most recently, epistemological anarchism, a result of
strident post-modernism. In the first case, human experience is
reduced to overt and measurable categories, actions, or dispositions. The fields of psychology and psychiatry are now replete with
such reductionisms, from the arid descriptions of dysfunctional
behavior in the *Diagnostic and Statistical Manual* of the American
Psychiatric Association, to the legions of randomized trials, cor-

relational studies, and survey results that undergird mainstream psychology. A person is not a person in these purviews, but an aggregate, a statistic, which can conveniently be treated like any other statistic at any other time and place. Hence, for example, a client of mine recently visited an HMO psychiatrist to find out about anti-depressant medication. This was a bright and sensitive woman who had been dealt a brutal hand in childhood. One of her main battles was to be heard, seen, and recognized as a valuable and self-determining person. As she reported it, however, her psychiatrist treated her in just the opposite fashion. He offered little time, listened selectively to her words, and abruptly drew conclusions about her condition. Instead of the warmth, caution, and attunement that *should* have obtained from this so-called health expert, he provided a cold and calculated pronouncement as to her "disability." According to my client, the psychiatrist told her that, based on authoritative evidence, she had a "chronic" condition that will require life-long medication. Not only did this pronouncement precipitate an acute (and what seemed to me, justifiable) episode of outrage on the part of my client, but it also deeply reverberated with her feelings of worthlessness and impotency. Fortunately, and following some highly intense encounters, we were able to demystify in our therapy some of the perceptions she had gleaned from her psychiatric visit, and she was eventually able to regain some sense of control; she also became, but for a few brief exceptions, medication-free. Many other clients, however, may not have such opportunities to debrief following similar experiences—and there are numerous similar experiences in my view.

Spiritual puritanism has a very long history that predates behavioral reductionism. Spiritual puritanism, as it is often expressed in contemporary psychology, has two basic dimensions—anti-materialism and elitist transcendentalism. Spiritual puritanism de-emphasizes the bodily, downplays the disorderly, and disdains the primeval. In spiritual puritanism, there is very little of the dark, the carnal, and the disorderly and very much of the visible, the rarified, and the contained or comforting. Spiritual puritanism is also often associated with transcendental

absolutism: the presumption that, in certain extraordinary circumstances, human consciousness can totally transcend its finite
trappings—the body, death, time and space, and so on. Although
tempered in recent years, spiritual puritanism is still evident, and
ever a threat, in a variety of occult and esoteric circles in psychology. The recent controversies surrounding "sages," gurus, and New
Age prophets attest to the continued power of spiritual puritanism
to wreak havoc. While I have written at length elsewhere regarding
this issue—particularly about the work of Ken Wilber—I will relate
several other anecdotes that illuminate my concern.[1]

A glance at much of the New Age spiritual literature today
reveals two things: It is of burgeoning interest and it sells. Books
with titles like *Unlimited Power, The Seven Spiritual Laws of Success,* and *A Brief History of Everything,* are cogent and sophisticated exemplars of the raging new trend. *New Age* magazine, the
upscale and fashionable voice for the above tradition recently displayed the headline, "Wipe out stress, pain, and anxiety: The right
bodywork can do it all." However, it is precisely the smoothness
and sophistication of these periodicals that concerns me. Bright
and articulate thinkers are asking increasing numbers of spiritual
seekers to move from inquiries about the sacred to assumptions
or even presumptions about the latter. Why do there have to be
"laws" about spirituality and success? How is it that spirituality is
even remotely related to conventional notions of "success," which
is what the author, Deepak Chopra, implies. As tongue in cheek
as Wilber can be, who is he to write a book about "everything"?—
and a "brief" history no less. Can we, as flesh and bones mortals
really inform ourselves about everything—this would be laugh-
able if it weren't taken so seriously by many readers.[2]

And yet we must ask, what is actually going on here that so
many are absorbing works such as those above with so much relish? What is at the core of the appeal? In my view, it is, again, the
promise of purity, of breaking away from the body, and of meld-
ing, irrevocably, with the Truth. Paul Tillich warned us about this
kind of polarizing; it is the same problem as polarizing generally—the problem of idol worship. Idol worship for Tillich is

one of the cardinal sins of human endeavor, and particularly of religious belief.[3] For Tillich, idol worship is demonization; it is the magnification of finite beings and objects into infinite beings and objects; or to put it another way, it is the mistaking of pieces of the holy for the holy itself. The implications of this view cannot be overstated, and are a cornerstone of this book. But with regard to spiritual puritanism, the problem of idol worship is all too evident today. It is notable in the ideologies that are propagated, in the objects (from temples to churches, medicines to "holy" lands) that are sacralized, and in the symbols and rituals that are fixated upon. It is not that such investitures lack worth in the human arena, or even the best of human arenas; it is just that they are misplaced. When investitures become fixated upon, they become exclusive, dangerous, and narrow. One need only look at the casualties—worldwide—emanating from cults, political ideologies, and religious sects to understand the force of this peril.

Another, but very different polar peril is strident post-modernism, or the position that all beliefs are foundationless, all reality is socially constructed, and all views are equivalent in their essential value. While there is great merit in much of the post-modern outlook, not the least of which are the critiques of reductionism and puritanism, as touched on above, there is also a lurking menace. This menace is the shadow side of Becker's psychology without consolation, and Tillich's theology without idolatry, and both theorists were aware of it. Friedrich Nietzsche, too, knew the problem well: if you take away the gods, what will you be left with? The point is that courageous confrontations with being, as all three theorists well knew, are very trying enterprises, and hence, very rarely tried. Those who have genuinely bucked the tide or rattled the foundations of their time were often persecuted for their positions, either by external imposition, or by impositions deep within themselves, within their physical, emotional, and cognitive cores. Today, however, some have forgotten these illuminating lessons. Again, with almost fanatical zeal, there are some who would deconstruct with abandon, who would mistake anarchy for freedom, and impulsivity for spontaneity. The result is that, as much as we have a society courting spiritualism and fundamentalism, we also have a society courting nihilism and anarchism.

Replacing one form of madness for another, however, will not work. I fear for the children growing up in our post-modernist cacophony; where will they learn emotional and intellectual depth, interpersonal commitment, and enduring values? At the risk of sounding like a reactionary here (which I definitely do not wish to do!), I am concerned about the increasing casualness of society—the quick fix and throwaway mentality. If you're feeling blue, pop a pill; if you disdain where you're living, go somewhere else; if you don't like your family tradition, adopt a new one; if you don't like what the government is doing, lose yourself on the Internet; if you're dissatisfied with live encounters, indulge in "chat rooms." If you don't like Western (or Eastern) values, make up your own, etc. Where are we going with all this haste, rearrangement, and impulse living, and for whose benefit? I fear that some of the very destinations that post-modern thinkers endeavored to avert (e.g., robotic living) we are headlong edging toward. These destinations also include but are not exhausted by selfishness, consumerism, ethnocentrism, and technocracy!

From my standpoint then, it is clear that a new psychology is needed. Such a psychology would incorporate the best that is offered by the aforementioned perspectives but steer between their excesses. It would be both systematic and yet flexible, practical yet daring. This is the psychology—science of humanity—to which this book aspires.

Toward an Awe-Based Psychology

If we start with awe, several points ring clear: First, psychology cannot simply stand as an isolated, fragmentary discipline. Psychology cannot confine itself to observable behavior or measurable constructs or regulatory mechanisms. By the same token, psychology cannot be reduced to electro-chemical processes originating in the brain, nor to cultural assumptions nor linguistic structures.

By contrast, to be a vibrant field, psychology must recognize the many layers of living that lie far beyond any one slice or compartment. Yet we must be careful here, lest we fall into the trap of the spiritual puritan or epistemological anarchist. Psychology is not itself a mysticism or a religion or a faith, although it may address these. Nor is psychology a foundationless, socially constructed language game.

To me psychology is above all an inquiry.[4] It is an inquiry into the innermost recesses of awareness, which include individual as well as collective, freeing as well as constraining, psychospiritual dimensions. As such, psychology must go beyond terms like diversified and complex to do its subject matter justice. It must go beyond even interdisciplinary or multi-faceted. Purely and simply, psychology must begin with awe.

In beginning with awe—humility and wonder—we have all the elements of a larger and more animated psychology. We have all the elements whereby the exploration, description, and interpretation of human lives can be assessed justly, wherever those processes and understandings may lead. While awe does not guarantee Truth (which in itself is contradictory to awe), it does guarantee sensitivity, effort, and fullness. This is the hallmark of psychological anthropology.[5]

The first principle of awe is appreciation. Appreciation is immersion, the setting aside of time, for that which is investigated. To appreciate an anxious individual, for example, I must stay with him for a concerted period. I must open my senses to him—my senses of taste, touch, and smell, as well as those of sight and sound. I must also open my feelings, imaginings, and intuitions to that person. Everything must be available. When I am with such a person, I want to know as much about him as possible—presenting problem, relevant history, concerns, struggles, and so on—but I also want to know how he is related to his body, environment, and world. What, if anything, does his anxiety have to do with living in a decaying body, drowning in a career, or floundering in a culture, all while perched perilously on a dying blue planet, hurtling endlessly through space? Hence, the kind of listening and seeing the latter requires is awe-based, appreciation-based, not only or necessarily information-based. If I look at my friend in parts, or dissect his character, I cannot access him in his "nakedness," his bruteness before life. If I do, I only get parts and pieces of my friend in return.

I believe appreciation can be applied to any area of psychology—developmental, social, physiological, research, even organizational, and administrative—with fruitful results. How many studies of psychological "functioning" must we revisit to infuse them with appreciation—how many deeper, fuller, more variegated results would we obtain?

By the same token, we cannot appreciate forever. Human beings are caught in that odd juxtaposition between being connected to and yet separated from all that we perceive. There comes a time when we become overwhelmed by all that we accompany. At these times, we need to pull back some, to clarify or digest what we have witnessed. Or there comes a point where we simply become curious about particular aspects of what we discover, and we desire to pursue those aspects. Whatever the case, a second principle that emerges from awe is discernment. To discern is to weigh, clarify, and ultimately affirm a given direction or value. As I accompany my anxious friend, I begin to notice certain features that distinguish his particular difficulty. A gestalt emerges. He is hunched over with a certain timidity, his voice quivers with a particular tonality—he is silent at distinct points, talkative at other points. All these qualities and many more help me to apprehend the shape or configuration of my friend's predicament. This shape can then be compared to other shapes that I have witnessed, both of my friend and others' in similar situations, and a general understanding can begin to be perceived.

Awe, appreciation, and discernment, then, can be highly beneficial conditions on which to base psychological knowledge. An awe-based psychology emerges not from book-learning, although it assuredly can benefit from that, but from an awakened sensitivity to life, an awakened sensitivity to creation itself. In the language of traditional science, an awe-based psychology draws upon the deepest possible sources to discover and verify[6] experiential data. It is not content with mere cognitive or behavioral inquiries, but with inquiries that embrace the whole person or whole subject matter, so far as that person or subject matter can be discerned. Correspondingly, measures, statistics, and other quantitative confirmations do not assuage an awe-based psychology. While awe-based psychology does not preclude these forms of confirmation, it considers them solely in the context of their resonance with individual lives, meanings, and experiences. Awe-based psychology is therefore an amalgamated psychology, maximally nuanced and encompassing.

The move from awe to appreciation to discernment requires a learning style and life philosophy that psychology—as with many other disciplines—has yet to substantially embrace. Yet there is a great need for psychology and related disciplines to embrace such a learning style, to address core human problems, and to promote sweeping discoveries, hunches, and theories. At the same time, there is also a need for psychology and related disciplines to acknowledge the paltriness of their discoveries, and the wisdom to question and revise them in the light of new evidence. As previously suggested, finally, there is a need for psychology and related fields to adopt a telescopic stance toward human experience, but also a view that is firmly anchored to individuals, to innermost loves, fears, and sorrows. The fluid center, I propose, is one such basis on which to ground psychology.

The Fluid Center: A Definition

The fluid center is any sphere of human consciousness which has as its concern the widest possible relationships to existence; or to put it another way, it is structured inclusiveness—the richest possible range of experience within the most suitable parameters of support.

The fluid center begins and unfolds through awe, the humility and wonder of living. It is precisely through awe that we come to know how daunting life is, and how readily our presumptions crumble; and yet, conversely, it is precisely through awe that we are awakened to life's majesty, and how dramatically our despair is misplaced. Somewhere in that dynamism is vivacity—the heart, soul, and core of which is both fluid and central.

To illustrate the fluid center, reflect upon the rich and contrasting elements in a work of jazz, a love relationship, or a Vincent van Gogh painting. The jazz begins with a form, let us say a classical melody, but then weaves and wends its way into new forms, broader melodies. Similarly, a love relationship opens with some form of physical attraction. Eventually, however, it manifests in many other forms, for example, emotional and spiritual attraction, a sense of shared values, and a sense of connectedness with life. Van Gogh's paintings, such as his series on sunflowers, start with the simple outline of its subject. Upon closer inspection, however, they connote a great deal more—a sense of vibrancy, hopefulness, and aliveness. To further envision a fluid center, take any particular form or configuration of consciousness and consider its degree of vibrancy, dynamism, and intensity. Consider the ways in which it interrelates with other centers of consciousness and other forms.

The fluid center is a pause, a pivot point, and a space between. It veers between constraint (structure, reticence) on the one hand and expanse (spontaneity, brashness) on the other. It can be both inner and outer, physical and mental, or it can emphasize only one of these self-dimensions. Choice is the fulcrum of the fluid center. Choice requires both centeredness—focus, accommodation—and fluidity—range, exploration. The degree to which a person or society experiences choice within their particular center, largely determines their extent of discernment, solidity, and depth. Further, choice promotes the ability to flow in and out of and enlarge one's center of awareness. To the degree that a person or society lacks choice, they are likely to be either rigidly centered or impulsively fluid. It is likely that discernment would play a minimal role in such a circumstance and that drivenness, panic, or inertia would play the dominant roles. It is difficult to be discerning, for example, if one is hammered by power, cowed by authority, or paralyzed by unpredictability. Conversely, to the extent that one is inured to vulnerability, hateful to accommodation, or aghast at limitation, one's discernment is also impaired.

There is no objective means by which to determine the legitimacy, usefulness, or appropriateness of a given center of consciousness. Only the party or parties affected by such consciousness can determine its value, and only those parties affected should be consulted as to its value. Do such parties experience an optimal degree of freedom, richness, and nourishment within their centers of consciousness? Are their centers of consciousness respectful of other centers of consciousness with which they may interact? Only the marketplace of experience—dialogue, reflection—will even begin to settle such matters. Still, there is much that we can glean presently from the vision of a fluid center and that is what we shall proceed to elucidate.

We will begin then with the prototype upon which consciousness in its many manifestations is based—the developing child.

2

The Fluid Center in Personality and Development

> For after all, what is man in nature? A nothing in regard
> to the infinite, a whole in regard to nothing, a mean be-
> tween nothing and the whole; infinitely removed from
> understanding either extreme....What shall he do then
> but discern somewhat of the middle of things...?
>
> —Blaise Pascal (*Pensées*, 1654)[1]

Let us surmise the following: From the moment a fetus perceives, it experiences both form and formlessness.[2] While the precise onset of fetal perception is controversial, one point strikes clear: Throughout its unfolding, the child is both contained and free, both centered (anchored) in its environment and fluid. It is centered in its surroundings (i.e., womb), but it is also to some extent buoyant, pliable, and dynamic within those confines. It is dependent on the support of its host, and yet it is also minimally differentiated from its host, as demonstrated by its ability to stretch or kick. Eventually, the fetus may even be able to experience independent mood states (i.e., irritability) and communicate—albeit crudely—within the womb.

Yet little, it appears, prepares the fledgling for the rude awakening—the explosive alteration—of birth itself. The being at this juncture is thrown, jabbed, and battered into existence. It emerges bloodied, shaken, and stunned. At the same time, however, the newborn is remarkably protected during this turbulent journey. From the moment of expulsion, for example, it travels through the birth canal, onto awaiting arms, into a loving embrace. Virtually instinctively, the caretaker caresses the neonate, pulls her to her breast, and gently strokes her. If there are glimpses of the outer world during these moments, they are but fleeting snatches—flashing gasps for air, sparkling receptions of light, brief stirrings of limbs. On the whole, however, from the swaddling to the soothing, the baby is (and emphatically needs to be) enveloped in warmth.

Given this sequence of events then, we can surmise the following: However strong the desire for autonomy, the earliest infantile needs are for safety, structure, and security. There is a direct parallel, moreover, between these early needs and R.D Laing's notion of ontological security.[3] From the standpoint of ontological security, not only do infants require supportive physical structures but they also require a sense of being grounded in existence itself. They need to feel loved, in other words, and not merely feel that their overt needs will be taken care of. They need to feel that they are more than somebody's sense of duty, obligation, or fulfillment, but that they are special before creation, a substantive being who holds weight in the world. Finally, it is out of these experiences that children develop a sense of existential containment, hope, and trust.

There is, of course, a very wide gradient with respect to ontological security. It can range from the comforting forms described above, to the confining, impinging, or even absent structures associated with dysfunction; and it can range from the inert and complacent to the vital and dynamic. While much of this terrain has already been eloquently plumbed, much mystery remains. For example, Bateson, Laing and others have closely charted the communication patterns of "schizophrenogenic" families; Bowen and McGoldrick have explored the transmission of dysfunctional family myths; and numerous researchers have elucidated the microprocesses of infant-caretaker interactions and their implications for later functioning.[4] Yet, to my knowledge, there has not been a cohesive synthesis of these findings, and there are still many regions left unexplored. What follows is a very limited attempt to pull together recent developmental data and my own personal and clinical understanding. Specifically, I will propose some of the key processes that, in my view, are associated with optimal ontological security or the fluid center. To illustrate my perspective, I will present Toby, a composite character who reflects a typical but traumatized American youth.

Roots, Routes, and Patterns

Over the course of a given childhood, there are innumerable means through which centeredness and fluidity, form and vitality, are shaped. As both a father and a therapist, I have been privileged to observe some of these operations at a very close range. What is immediately striking to me—as alluded to above—is not only how quickly the shaping process begins, but also how pervasively it spreads. In Western culture in particular, there is a hasty premium placed on boundaries, rules, and restraints in the infant-caretaker nexus. The drive on the part of the child to explore, to play, and to absorb the world about her is often relegated to a secondary status in our culture. On the other hand, the need to conform to rules, to develop habits, and to adapt to routines in our society is frequently viewed as primary.[5] It is evident that if a culture requires a certain superstructure to operate, then it will summarily demand that its offspring adapt to this superstructure. It is for this reason that so much emphasis is placed on mechanized learning in our culture, and that speed, instant results, and overt knowledge are so highly prized. Be that as it may, my chief question here concerns human liberation. While it is clear that a degree of centering—shaping, structuring, supporting—is necessary for primary ontological security, how much is optimal? What forms of centering optimize our relationships with existence—our sense of separation and connection, freedom and responsibility, and meaning and purpose? Where do we begin our examination of these issues?

The chief source for answers is not only in the developmental literature, but also in our own careworn hearts. What is it that we see when confronted with an array of maturation styles? Let me elaborate.

There is on the part of children a need for the predictable. When this predictability falters, the child, too, in some sense wavers. If I fail to regularly and reliably put my three year old to sleep, his sleep cycle lapses. If I omit washing his hands, he ceases to be concerned about dirt. If I neglect to challenge his acquisitiveness, he acquires at will, and so on. Further, it is increasingly evident to

.... that he not only needs but solicits my wife and me to set firm boundaries periodically and to guide him and let him know which of his actions can be relied on and which can't, what can be played with and what must be taken seriously, what can support him or what might endanger him. But I am equally convinced that far too much is made of such programming and admonishments in our culture. In too many households there is a continual pressure to conform, to please, and to succeed. In too many households parental authority saps the life out of children, or it is engaged with fear, resentment, or hysteria. The plea cannot be overemphasized that children need magic in their lives—ecstasy, wonder, and adventure—as much as they need structure and protection. They need to gaze at stars, ask questions about the dead, and explore dark places. It needs to be made much more clear, particularly in our culture, that there is more to life than business suits and shopping carts, or play-dates and video stores. To see and feel the natural world, to wonder, and to share those sensibilities with sympathetic companions is one of the lasting legacies of childhood.

But let me be clear here: I am not upholding some banal form of liberal parenting. Nor am I speaking about an "anything goes" household, in which children, pets, and caretakers run amok; nor am I endorsing a saccharine, superficial, or cavalier household. I am speaking about a full and deep encounter with children, an encounter that stretches limits, to be sure, but also one that provides the limits to stretch. The kind of contact that I envision here has many levels of nurture—from protection, affection, and gentleness, to evocation, challenge, and guidance.

While not incompatible with contemporary developmental theory, the dynamics above must be seen in a fuller light. Contemporary developmental theory focuses chiefly on family interactions; it does not largely account for the systemic nature of those interactions, the parts of those interactions that are bound up with the culture, the ecology, and the cosmos. While some theorists—e.g., social constructionists and transpersonalists—are attempting to redress the aforementioned omissions, much more needs to be elaborated from the standpoint of the fluid center.

From a fluid center view, then, children's development (in conjunction with temperament) is mediated by three key elements—verbal, tacit, and observational learning. Verbal learning is conducted through vocalization and language; tacit learning is conveyed through sensation and intuition; and observational learning is inculcated through imitation and modeling.[6]

The great parental challenge, of course, is how to optimize these three elements, how to facilitate them with the zest, grace, and dynamism that I have illustrated above. All three elements, in other words, are likely to have a fundamental and enduring impact on a child. They are likely to reflect a level of warmth, vibrancy, and empowerment that can either enhance a child's ability to move out into the world, or, in the absence of such conditions, betray a level of tension, confusion, and anxiety that thwarts the child's every step. The issue, however, is far from simple, and requires a consideration of the interplay of each of the key elements of mediation. Consider:

The degree to which a caretaker or parent can speak clearly and respectfully to a child is dependent on a vast and unappreciated number of variables. In addition to the parent's level of education and her ability to articulate herself, many questions must be asked about her underlying emotionality, such as the degree to which she experiences fear, volatility, or regret. Any one of these emotions can affect the way she speaks, from the pervasive use of negative declarations, e.g., "no," "can't," and "don't," to the repeated employment of sarcasm, mocking, or denigration. To be sure, this language style results in part from the early conditioning of the parent and from that of the parent's parent and so on; but equally, I contend, it stems from the parent's current conditioning and circumstances. Let us look more closely at such conditioning and circumstances as we witness them today.

On a consistent and daily basis in contemporary America, our parent is likely to encounter a surge of entanglements—from oppressive vocational obligations to spiritless social enmeshments to withering technical preoccupations. Enter the banks, real estate offices, and computer outlets; witness the clothing chains, technology shops, and pharmacies; peruse the homes, apartments, and shopping malls across this great continent, and you will see the interplay of the above problems. You will see the man on his cell phone blustering through traffic. You will see the woman in the department store gliding through rows of designer jeans. You will see the hordes of teenagers "raving" or gorging on MTV. You will see potbellied young managers ensnarled by deadlines, teachers mired in oversize classes, nurses addled by understaffing, and doctors surfeited by paperwork. You will see waiters and flight attendants, bus drivers and repairpersons, service attendants and maintenance workers, line workers and day laborers going through countless motions, logging countless clock hours. And you will see legions searching for work or trembling about being laid off or sweating about being cut from their insurance rolls. In short, you will see a sobering portrait of American life. This is a life that, for all its virtues, too often compresses, intrudes, and devitalizes; that bullies, hordes, and indulges; that dazes and disorients; and that slothfully "gets by."

What are we to say about the effects of such fragmenting and polarizing in our midst? How do they impact on parents, children, development? The impact is cumulative, structural and, too often, insidious. The impact is cumulative because whatever else may weigh on parents, pushing buttons all day or filling out forms or kissing up to one's boss will assuredly not lighten their load. The oppressive regimentation and accommodation of everyday life can associate with impotency for many parents. It can give them a sense of unrelenting smallness, meaninglessness, and insignificance. This sense of meagerness is then passed on to their children, whether through denigrating words, prostrating expressions, or general uneasiness. On the other hand, some parents polarize in the direction of anger, frustration, and vengefulness. Their reaction to belittlement in daily life is to "stick it" to belittlement. While they may not express this attitude publicly, for fear of retribution, they may well unleash it in the home, where bystanders are helpless. They may vent their rage through intimidation, aggrandizement, drinking, or drug-taking, or they may physically or sexually assault others.

Whatever their mode, tacit or verbal, bombastic or resigned, the message of these parents to their children is clear: "You are helpless, you have no value beyond that to which I consent, and your life prospects are dim." In turn, the child begins to feel rage, or the suppression of it, and he, too, contingent on temperament, is likely to perpetuate the abusive cycle.

The most pervasive form of polarization in our culture, however, may be much less visible than those described above, yet doubly insidious. I propose that it is the dull midpoint between constrictive and expansive extremes. This midpoint or homeostasis is probably the most common contemporary personality style. The reason for this commonality in our culture is our genius for promoting it. While a minority of people become despairingly hopeless and contracted, and a smattering of others become hysterically tyrannical and inflated, the vast majority simply "adjust." Day by day, these adjusted encroach on American life, and era by era they eclipse the globe. The shift toward the mass—mass culture, mass marketing, and mass production—has almost entirely enveloped contemporary consciousness. The key to this consciousness is the path of least resistance. Whatever is handiest, smoothest, and least complicated is what leads. This is a mentality that appeals to our laxest impulses and that squarely aligns with our late-capitalist consumerism. It is a mentality that seduces, tricks, and ultimately deludes.

It deludes by misleading, and it misleads by making profound experiences—e.g., sex, spirituality, freedom—appear to be facile experiences, experiences without struggle or weight. Take freedom. Many of us think we are free, e.g., from want, tyranny, and oppression, but is this really so, and for whom (certainly not the disadvantaged)? We who are privileged (e.g., white, middle class) enjoy some liberty, but to what degree and in what form? We are free to vote, but for whom—the latest billionaire, media darling, or party sycophant? We are free to live on credit but at what price: anger, indebtedness, distress? We are free to choose our lifestyle, but with what burdens: mortgages, high-interest loans, sixty-hour work weeks? We are free to pursue happiness, but through what means:

fast food, beer, cigarettes, and television? We are free to express our individuality, but within what range: 100 to 130 pounds, a dose of Prozac, designer clothes? So yes, we do enjoy an initial level of freedom in our society; neither kings nor dictators reign over us. But we hardly have time to savor our hard-won liberation, or when we can savor it, it is deceptively narrow.

The problem with the adjusted or competent center is that life is lived largely through others—other things, other ideas, other power. Life is lived at a muted level—contained, manageable, and occasionally adventurous, but it is adventurous in controlled and vicarious ways. It is adventurous through videos, recreational drugs, or surfing the Net. It is bold through sex scandals, political intrigues, and the latest hype about staying youthful or discovering one's true identity in six easy lessons. Or it is empowering through a cult hero, a religious figure, or an athlete. But less and less is life animated through personal discovery, intimacy with others, or self-reflection. While life has become more manageable for many people, it has become commensurately less engaged. (See for example, Joseph Royce's apt description of "encapsulated man." Many today are fluid, but their fluidity is vicarious, mediated, or, in short, encapsulated. Practically an entire life today can be lived through a cubicle).[7]

Despite this disturbing trend, why is it that poll results characterize Americans as "happy" or "content?" When jobs are "plentiful," and the economic forecast is positive, how can I complain? Indeed, if I took the superficial mentality of poll results at face value, I should be ashamed of my analysis. However, I don't do this because I believe that poll results (as well as general surveys) reflect the very mentality which I am critiquing. I don't really believe one discovers much from these data-gathering behemoths, and I believe conversely that one can discover a lot more about people by interacting with people, by opening to the "people" in oneself, and by closely observing, intuiting, and recording one's experience of people. The richer, rounder, stories are etched in people's faces, in the local tales that they tell, and in the art, literature, and music that they produce. And what these sources tell me is that there is a storm gathering in our midst. It is not, but for occasional exceptions, a graphic or overt storm, and it may take decades to burst, but its character is palpable now. It is manifest in hollowness, indifference, and self-contempt. It is manifest in a culture that worries more about its stock options than its teachers and its sport utility vehicles more than its emotional or physical health. But the story does not end there; as in every great drama (and our lives certainly qualify), there is a counter-position on the horizon, and it must not be short-changed.

Spirals of Development

Most people live, whether physically, intellectually or morally, in a very restricted circle of their potential being. They *make use* of a very small portion of their possible consciousness, and of their soul's resources in general, much like a man who, out of his whole bodily organism, should get into a habit of using and moving only his little finger. Great emergencies and crises show us how much greater our vital resources are than we had supposed.

—William James (*Letters of William James*, 1920)[8]

Development is akin to a spiral. We are spiral-like as fetuses, and our consciousness spirals out from the womb. At first, our spirals are miniscule and tentative. We twist and stretch our musculature, for example, or we inch to and from our crib. But the spiraling process is much subtler than simple physical movements. In time, we venture out from the security of our emotions, our imagination, and our language—we break into new forms of acting, perceiving, and communicating. We try out new moral frameworks, new friendships, and new worldviews. And our circle widens.

Like ships at sea, however, we virtually always return to our points of departure, our harbors, and our safe domains. We are enriched by our journeys, enlarged, but we must also face our limits and needs for grounding. While the compass of our humanity expands, it also bends back on itself, furling and unfurling, cycling and recycling into ever changing trajectories. "Individual…development," writes Guidano,[9] "should be regarded as a *hortogenic progression*, meaning that it is an open-ended, spiraling process in which the continuous reordering of selfhood dynamics results in the emergence of more structured and integrated patterns of internal complexity" [italics in original].

The great question, of course, is what is the quality of one's structured and integrated patterns?—Are they vibrant and alive, or are they muted and inert? Are they anchored and bound, or frayed and adrift? Open and flexible, or blocked and constrained? We will now take up such inquiries.

As human beings grow, we internalize a vast array of socio-cultural patterns. These patterns interact with the naturally unfolding patterns of our genes, physiology, and temperaments. Taken together, the patterns of our experience are composed of many intricate routes. By routes, I mean modes or directions of experience, like the feelings, thoughts, or sensations we perceive, the impressions made by our environments, and the people, things, and ideas we encounter. From the moment of conception, I would surmise, the routes of experience begin to bud. These routes—or, more properly at the earliest stages, "capillaries"—of experience may associate with a wealth of basic conditions: from the viability of the fertilized egg, to the immediate physical environment of the egg, to the psychological condition of the mother hosting the egg.[10] As the zygote develops into a fetus (about the eighth week), the capillaries of experience presumably proliferate, prefiguring their mature, postnatal state.

By the fifth month of development, the fetus encounters—and must negotiate—a staggering array of impressions. For example, to what degree can the fetus relax in its intrauterine home? To what degree does its physical development preclude relaxing and require tensing, jostling, or fighting? To what extent does the mother—its host—welcome the emergence of the fetus? To what degree does she embrace it, call to it, and reassure it? How do all the myriad forces outside the mother act on the fetus? What are the effects of automobile exhaust, cold from winter weather, or dust from old furnishings? What of the emotional climate? How do fears, criticisms, and frustrations affect the mother, and thereby become transferred to the fetus? How does the mother's relationship with her husband, lover, family, or friends impact the fetus? What about the business climate with which she associates, or the religion, neighborhood, or town with which she affiliates? As can be seen, the intricacy of influence (or "imprinting") on prenatal life is mind-bending, and social science has only begun to unravel it.

The capillaries of experience, then, are of enormous developmental import. As the fetus emerges into infancy, those capillaries mature into full-blown routes, as I have suggested, and those routes, in turn, form the rudiments of infantile knowledge. For example, in her first few months, the infant discovers her mother, father, and immediate surroundings. She habituates to her body, and her bodily movements, and she familiarizes herself with the rhythms of darkness and light. She also begins to learn about her identity and the distinction between people and things. In short, the child's prenatal impressions merge with postnatal distinctions to forge adult articulations, habits and routines.

Yet articulations—as with routines and habits—are so often transitory in this life. The more the infant learns, the greater her encounter with mystery, uncertainty, and contradiction. For example, she awakens to the variations in her day-to-day environment, such as the appearance and disappearance of her caretakers and the changes in her diet. She finds that she feels warmth and comfort at one moment and chill and distress at another. She discovers the necessity for affection at one point and the urgency for activity-seeking at another. My point here is that the spirals of development are marked by many breaks, fissures, and disruptions. The routes of familiarity turn vague, obscure, or just plain incomprehensible at various points, and the infant is left suspended for brief periods of time.

Now, from developmental theory we know that as infants mature, they can readily assimilate many points of disruption. The infant discovers, for example, that the caretaker can still be in the environment even though he is removed from view, or that a modicum of unpredictability is part of living. These are the groundworks for what I have earlier called a competent center, a center (or ego) that is modestly adventurous but that knows when to rapidly pull in the reins and adjust. Piaget wrote a fair amount about such a center and so did Brazelton, Kohlberg, and even many of the neo-analytic theorists such as Mahler, Erikson etc.[11] The competent center is a culturally-desirable center, but too frequently it does not promote aliveness, inventiveness, or wonder. It helps people to "get along," but so often this getting along, as pointed to earlier, is associated with deep frustrations, which are then displaced on others.

The so-called bumps and bruises of ordinary living, then, are not psychology's major challenge—nor is the achievement of competency (although both have been perceived as such by very prominent developmental researchers). On the contrary, psychology's core task is to deeply illuminate our relationship to being—the vicissitudes of mystery—which underlie bumps, bruises, and competencies.

It is my thesis in this book that the competent or customary center is not a long-term solution for either individuals or society. Conventional developmental theory has wittingly or unwittingly played into the hands of this devitalized center through its stress on cognitive processes, brain development, and balanced or symmetrical interaction patterns. While these domains are valuable, they do not account for the vast uncharted substructure that underpins them. This substructure, which should command the lion's share of psychological developmental inquiry, is existence. The existential dimension of development is the innermost and furthermost context within which each of us develops. Beyond our electro-chemical processing, beyond our immediate environment, and beyond even our ancestry, we are all "thrown," as Heidegger put it, into an unfathomable venture. Each of us, at every moment, is but a speck in a cosmic process, the destination of which is inscrutable. Each person, each being, each cell, each element connects with countless other persons, beings, cells, and elements in both time and space. The question for development is to what extent are children enabled to encounter their cosmic predicament, or to what extent are they diverted from it—shielded, stunted, or crippled before it? The answer to this question bears directly on a child's sense of awe and on the evolving maturation of that sense: the fluid center.

Storm at the Center: Life-Transformation in a Typical American Child

As previously indicated, the patterns that navigate human development are laid down in intrauterine life, and they spiral out from there. To understand the nature and bases of these patterns, we must do more than formulate theories—we must animate lives. While there are a variety of ways to approach this task, I have chosen "Toby," a hypothesized case study, as my point of illustration. Toby (who is a composite of several lives with which I am familiar) is a typical American child, but then his life-trajectory begins to veer, and so too his range and depth of character. Accompany me now as we trace the markings of this change and the reformation it heralds for both Toby and society.

Toby has just been conceived. He is still in his mother, Jane's, womb, and he is the subject of great anticipation. Jane, however, cannot fully share her excitement about Toby. She cannot fully share or even afford to share her excitement about anything. There are many bases for this situation. Everyday, for example, Jane is hounded by bills she cannot pay. She is in a dead-end job as a clerical worker and barely makes enough for her and her husband, Edgar, to scrape by. To cope with this burden, and many others that she carries over from her earlier years, Jane indulges in alcohol. Several afternoons a week, and almost every evening, Jane ingests about a glass and a half of cheap cabernet to help her "chill out." She has struggled mightily to decrease this intake for fear that it will harm her fetus, but she is only sporadically successful.

When Jane goes to work, she feels trapped. Her boss is very

formal with her, and constantly pressures her to produce. She has very little time to chat or get to know the other employees, and she is frozen for most of the day before a computer.

Jane grew up in a middle-class Caucasian neighborhood in the late 1950s, was bright, and received a parochial education.

Throughout her life, Jane has felt oppressed. Her father was an aloof and humorless autocrat who "tolerated" his three children. Her mother was warmer toward her and her siblings, but was frequently fatigued. To cope with this chronic condition, Jane's mother became a prescription medication addict (not so different from the 90 million or so Americans who rely on these remedies today), and she virtually never participated in vigorous exercise.

Jane's husband, Edgar, is somewhat like Jane's father. Although he is wittier and more sociable than her father, he is often both rigid and distant. A 40-year-old computer salesman who spent half his adult life chasing women and drinking highballs, Edgar managed to complete college, but found little in the way of lasting or meaningful work. To Edgar, work is work and play is a weekend with "the boys" (his ex-college chums) driving golf balls. Edgar is exhausted on most days. He works for a large firm with adequate health and pension benefits, but there is hardly a day that he works fewer than nine hours. Edgar collects rare baseball cards and spends most of his evenings searching for them on the Internet.

Edgar's father was a medical technician and his mother a nurse. His father drank a moderate amount of beer and occasionally went on tirades. Although he was not, for the most part, physically abusive, he would occasionally shun Edgar and his younger brother or devalue their manhood. The father was generally "reasonable" according to Edgar, but he rarely made himself available to talk to the boys or to inquire about their interests. Edgar's mother was a caring and responsible nurse, but she was tense, as a whole, at home. She deeply resented her husband for his drinking and periodic outbursts, and she increasingly felt emotionally and physically impoverished.

These are but a few of the routes of Jane and Edgar's life as they contemplated bringing Toby into the world. Although Jane and Edgar's life was for the most part typical in modern day America, consider the intricate tracks they began to lay on their gestating boy—months before he was ready to emerge from the womb. For Jane, the prospect of celebrating and joyously affirming her little offspring was abruptly and repeatedly squelched. Money, lack of esteem, frustration with her husband, and anger at father figures in her life perpetually ate away at her. She was "happy enough" she told friends, but the "enough" part was a repeated and embodied barrier to her communication with Toby. Whenever she'd begin to lovingly "talk" to her prenatal son, she would immediately experience somatic tension. Her stomach would tighten, her throat became choked, her voice quivered, and her breathing contracted.

How would her fetus respond? We can only speculate, but it is likely that on many and diverse levels he would be impacted. And what would happen when dad (Edgar) appeared on the scene? How would tiny Toby react to his agitated gait, his manner of speaking, and his guarded gestures? What would Toby feel as Edgar greeted him in his flat, expressionless style? What would Toby sense as Edgar abruptly withdrew from dinner to "surf the net?" What would Toby feel from Jane at that point, and how would Jane communicate with Toby? What does Toby learn about the parameters of joy, stimulation, and comfort, or the encroachments of futility, tension, and fear?

The above patterns and paths that comprise them are as subtle as the formation of blood vessels throughout the human body. From capillaries to veins to arteries, the human organism comprises a vast network of vascular systems. To the degree that those systems are nourished, they are animated, energized, and empowered; to the degree that they are deprived, they become ossified, enfeebled, and inert. For Toby, the pathways of history, environment, and culture recapitulate the latter modality of deprivation more than the former dimension of nourishment—but he is hardly alone.

The implication in Jane and Edgar's experience with Toby is that so much of what we take for granted as normal child development is in fact twisted—riddled with blocks, deceptions, and distortions. The child comes to live in a cocoon of disability—from the debasements of culture and parents to the inner debasements of self. From the moment many children can feel, see, and hear, there are notable prohibitions on those modes. If you feel too much, you are shunned; if you see too much, you are blocked; if you touch too much, you are ostracized; if you hear too much you are avoided and so on. These ensnarling routes are learned very early and solidify as the child immerses in school, church, and other conventional settings. It is not that such children become pervasively dour or depressed; quite the contrary in many circumstances. What they do evolve into, however, is more like their parents—hampered in their range of expression, dulled in their ability to imagine, and stunted in their capacity to love. The routes of their existence become repetitive, entrenched, and constrained.

On the other hand, this conventional cocoon is protective and reassuring to many people. In the famous movie scene between Andre Gregory and Wallace Shawn in *My Dinner with Andre,* Wally (played by Wallace Shawn) protests to Andre (played by Gregory) that he cherishes his warm blanket and morning coffee, and that he, unlike Andre, does not want to have to wrestle with existential questions for the remainder of his life. I am sympathetic with this view. Indeed, many who derive from relatively secure economic backgrounds aspire to it; but as a mantra for Western living? This does not work for me, nor for the many who live lives of quiet desperation.

Toby's self then emerges as a normative self, or to use the lexicon of social constructivism, a "bounded" self.[12] The well-bounded self has many advantages with regard to safety, security, and ease of function, but little suppleness, intensity, or passion. To the degree that Toby lives within preset boundaries, readily accommodates to others, and mechanically goes about his life, he will adapt and get through, but he will also pay many costs—both mental and physical—and so will his society.

Break in the Spiral/Tear in the Fabric

Thus far, we have explored Toby's normative world. Toby is a typical American child sustained by a typical family context. So long as Toby "gets along," for example, he will build what developmental researchers call "basic trust" with his caretakers, achieve the necessary degree of autonomy, and become adequately productive, competent, and generative. But what would happen if Toby's world were to collapse, if there was a rupture in his life-design? To what degree would conventional theorizing hold up in such circumstances? To what degree would it even be relevant? While many theorists have explored unusual or "abnormal" development, to be sure, few have explored its cosmic or existential dimensions. Few have peered into the world-shaking depths that might only be called poetic, religious, or metaphysical.[13] Consider, for example, how a loss, a death, or a cataclysmic event might impact Toby, say, at four years of age. Let us say that Toby's father, problematic as he may have been, was to die. Consider all the initial changes that would likely follow: Toby would feel upended—dazed and stunned. He would feel punished, abandoned, and discarded. He would fantasize about being culpable in some way, or implicate others, such as his loved ones, in the culpability. He would look about his life as if into an abyss. Objects, once vibrant and alive, would now appear petrified: a baseball glove, a book, his father's pinstripe shirt. He would cry the pang of a newborn wrested from his delivering mother. He would become maudlin, apathetic, and faithless. Anything or anyone he could rely on, he would fear he may lose. He would gaze into his mother's vacant eyes and wonder: "How can she manage on her own, let alone support me?" He might even begin to distrust his mother and to implicate her in his father's death. To the degree that she is ambivalent about that death, his distrust would grow.

At the same time, Toby might also feel a sense of pleasure—however fleeting—in his father's demise. He might experience relief, for example, from his father's periodic broods. He might even experience a degree of vindication in his dad's death, as if he deserved it, somehow, as a payback for his negligence; or he might feel angry toward his dad for dying—for committing the ultimate act of negligence. He might begin to wonder about death, about where his dad has gone, what form he has taken, and whether or not he could contact him. He might also wonder about his own life and death, about illness and decay, injury and destruction. How safe is the world, he might think, if a big, strong protector simply disintegrates?

Here one moment, gone the next.

Beyond what Toby initially experiences, however, and a key question for his development is how he (and others) will *respond* to his lot? From the standpoint of the fluid center, Toby has little precedence for the turmoil that besets him. His world is askew. Routes once familiar—a stable, if less than congenial dad, a reliable mom, a cohesive family unit, and so on—have all unraveled. The circle of Toby's rituals, routines, and possibilities, have all been fractured. His entire identity, scarred and delimited though it was, has become a heap of twisted strands.[14]

In the parlance of the seafarer, Toby has undergone a "hull breach." The world that was once remote, other, unknown, has abruptly crashed in. In the wake of this rupture, new feelings and images pour through Toby—perceptible in his gait, his speech, and his play. He is like a listing ship or a twig in a raging storm. Startlingly, all of the primal elements—wind, darkness, thunder—acquire renewed significance for Toby. Although unnerving to most children as they grow up, these elements acquire menacing new proportions for Toby. He hears a sound and imagines an intruder. He witnesses a repairman and mistakes him for a "giant." His dreams teem with primal imagery: devouring wolves, chattering skeletons, and creeping snakes. Scowling witches haunt his bedroom windows.

Each of these transformations echoes the rips, tears, and splinters in Toby's universe. Each is a stand-in for Toby's trepidation. By trepidation I mean terror of being—anxiety—and not merely localized fear. Toby is terrorized by the unfathomable—the immense, the loud, and the obscure. He is alarmed by the unruly, the unpredictable, and the disarrayed, and he is daunted by the subtle, the intuitive, and the shadowy.

To put it structurally, Toby is both centerless—awash, awhirl—and hypercentered—stifled, reduced—in the wake of his father's death. He is centerless because he no longer experiences a reliable ground in his life; all is thrown into question; all is in flux.

Toby is hypercentered, correspondingly, because he is stunned, staggered, and compressed before the challenges of fate. With jarring suddenness, for example, Toby is awakened to nature's astonishing forces. Like Blake before him, he senses "the wrath of the lion," the "howling of wolves," and the "raging of the stormy sea" in the upheaval of his grief.[15] He stretches and strains in all portions of his being. He stirs to emotions—fury, betrayal, melancholy—that he never quite previously faced (at least postnatally).

He discovers thoughts, images, and reveries that plow completely new ground—new conceptions about death, destruction, and vulnerability, new ideas about personal and parental power, and new perspectives on material reality. He forms novel relationships to objects, peers, and loved ones. His play and fantasy repertoires explode. He makes up a swarm of games and stories, for example, and he talks to himself incessantly while enacting them. He craves more fairy tales, hero stories, and yarns about war; he forms new relationships with pets, animals, and imagined playmates. He becomes more perplexed and inquisitive about existence, and he ceases taking things at face value and begins to reflect on their broader meanings.

Physically, he is besieged by uncomfortable sensations—such as a racing heart, a churning stomach, and a hunched back. He runs and jumps more, and the bolting deer becomes his twin.

Toby learns about filling gaps in his broken universe. If his dad is not there to guide or support him, and if his mom is preoccupied by grief, who but Toby must rise to the challenge? Who but Toby must learn about mobilizing, taking charge, and scavenging for what he needs? In this sense Toby must "become" his father. He must learn the painful lesson of the orphan, that *he* and not others are the bottom line and that if he wishes something to happen, then he's got to make it happen.

By implication then, Toby is thrust out into the world and forced to manage in ways that would have been unimaginable had tragedy not befallen him. He is called to recreate himself and to creatively respond to myriad levels of uncertainty. Without his father's frame, Toby is called to develop fresh conceptions of boyhood, of playing, fighting, and fraternizing. All that his father modeled for him must now be refashioned.

At the same time that he must cope with a dizzying new set of possibilities, however, he must also cope with the despair and sense of smallness that they create. For every moment that Toby expands into new avenues, he encounters equivalent moments where he feels overwhelmed, impotent, and inconsequential. The very same rupture that gives him opportunities to enlarge also presents him with new desires to shrink. In short, Toby discovers contraction. He cavorts with shadows, concealment, and silence.

As Toby contracts, objects, people, and the world look bigger to him—they *are* bigger from his angle. That which seems incidental to an average boy—noises, crowds—seems monstrous to Toby. For Toby, they are one more sign of the roiling, rumbling, and rippling within.

The Kinship With Classic Horror

It is no accident that trauma brings awareness of the macabre. Horror tales—especially the classic ones—give vent to our starkest experiences of life: grief, anguish, terror.[16] At the same time, however, these very same tales open us up to life, transport us to its further reaches, and immerse us in its wonders.

Tragedy is a paradox—there is no simple way around it. The more that someone is shaken, crushed, torn, the more he or she is initiated into a broader and deeper realm, a realm of torments and sufferings to be sure, but also of subtlety and force. There is no guarantee, of course, that a person will (or can) absorb such a world. Indeed, in our culture, there is every reason to believe that one will lack such a capacity. Where, for example, can people in the Western world go to cry, to decompress, or to rail at the universe? How many places can people go to fully and supportively unravel? I would argue that although scarce historically, such places may be even less available today.[17] Even long-term depth psychotherapy (one of the conventional sacred spaces) is threatened and embattled.

It is in this context of collapse that art horror stands in relief. By "art" or "classic" horror, I do not mean films or books that feature cheap thrills or visceral highs. I mean time-honored dramas that illustrate the multidimensionality of suffering. I mean stories—biblical, gothic, novelistic—that address horror's symbolism, its subtle as well as gross implications. Take the biblical story of Job, for example. Far from being about a simple miscreant who stumbles upon misfortune, Job is about the human encounter with absurdity. Job suffers, not because of who he is or what he's done, but because we all eventually suffer; we all eventually come up against the "monstrosities" of mayhem and death. The question for art horror (as it was for Job) is what is at the root of our suffering, and how are we to respond to it?

As with the protagonists in horror narratives—Toby is hammered by being. Toby's loss is existential far more than it is familial, behavioral, or even emotional. The death of a loved one—especially if it is faced—strips away the illusion of containment; it unveils life's infinity. This infinity is the great secret that classic writers of the macabre betray—if only we could perceive it. Horror tales remind us that we are all broken to one degree or another, we are all victims of life's puzzles. Following his father's death, Toby identifies with a legion of "puzzles"—from Frankenstein, to Dracula, to Phantom of the Opera. For example, Toby relates to Frankenstein's drive to transcend death through his monster, as well as his monster's rage at being abandoned. Toby resonates with Dracula's dark and brooding moods, his anonymity, and his craftiness. He also admires Dracula's "secret knowledge"—his commerce with ghosts, animals, and magic. At the same time, Toby also fears Dracula. He sees in him the menacing side of his father whom he fears will restore himself to life. Toby empathizes with the loneliness of the Phantom of the Opera. He sees in the Phantom's underground his own rich fantasy world and refuge from life. He also relates to the Phantom's deathly appearance and his capacity, like Dracula, to traverse and command the underworld.

Monstrosity reflects the break, the opening, the tear in the fabric of familiarity. Like actual tragedies, monster tales take us where "we are not supposed to go," where "transgressions" occur, and where humans should not "meddle." The monster is the part that goes "haywire," that takes us to our mental and physical limits—be those microcosmic and occult or macrocosmic and overt.

But monster tales unveil a great deal more. They cover the entire trajectory of crisis—from trauma to devastation to renewal and potential recovery. Accompany me now as we illuminate Toby's odyssey through this trajectory.[18] At the start of every horror classic, there is almost invariably a catastrophe. For Frankenstein this catastrophe was the premature death of his mother in childbirth; it was also the inability of technology to control death. For Dracula, the catastrophe was a war against an ancient enemy. For the Phantom, the disaster was his alienating deformity. And so on. The initial tragedy is the opening break in the spiral of living. This break alerts the protagonist—Frankenstein, Dracula, the Phantom, (Toby, us)—to the paltriness of our existence, but it also, by contrast, alerts us to the immense terrain—that "foreign country" as Shakespeare put it in *Hamlet*—that surrounds and encircles the paltriness. By "foreign country," I don't simply mean death—I mean the complex symbol of death. It is that which is radically other, taboo, and beyond—it is infinitude. Hence, it is not so much literal or physical death but radical change that gives birth to monsters or monstrous figures. When Frankenstein loses his mother, it is not simply a family tragedy; it is the shattering of a world, the evisceration of a presence, and the eradication of a bond that cannot be tidily restored. When Erik the Phantom becomes deformed, it is not just the "death" of his former attractiveness that is at stake; it is the annihilation of his sense of self, his sense of being, that matter most. That which classic horror illuminates then is the depth and breadth of the experience of tragedy. Classic horror gets right down to the guts of our suffering and takes death to its furthest and least palatable conclusions; it conveys to us that we are death, that we decay as we breathe, and that until we grapple with this paradox, we are as pitiable as the creatures we pity.

It is against this background of meagerness and ineptitude, helplessness and desperation, that monstrosity breeds. It is out of the quagmire of desolation that a beast awakens and is poised to uncoil. Victor Frankenstein's yen to extend life, Dracula's thirst for blood, and the Phantom's obsession with belonging all attest to the anguish at suffering's core—and the lengths to which we will go to obliterate that anguish. Toby, too, has become desperate. His father's death has ripped the heart out of his identity and brought him face to face with his (our) nothingness before creation. Therefore, he, too, may resort to extremities. These extremities can be detected at first in his night terrors and primal wails; later, they may become manifest in his fascination with guns or "bad" people; and still later, they may become apparent in his transformation into a "bad" person (a "monstrosity") himself—at least this is sometimes how the cycle unfolds.

At a recent holiday fair, a distraught 23-year-old caused a major stir. He was playing at one of the carnival booths when another young man stepped up and competed with him for a stuffed "tweety bird." Both youths, according to the newspaper account,[19] felt that they were eligible for the prize bird, but only one such prize was available. Refusing to settle for the alternative prize, another stuffed animal, each of the youths proceeded to scuffle with one another. Moments later, the 23-year-old pulled out a gun and started to shoot wildly, not only into his competitor, however, but at the crowd around him. By the time the gunfire ended, eight people were left wounded, and the mayhem unleashed a stampede.

In another twist of events, seven high school students, all during the years 1998–1999, slaughtered dozens of their classmates with automatic weapons. Several of these youths complained of being rejected by girlfriends, parents, and even a teacher.

Now here is a question for developmental psychology: How

do people arrive at these macabre junctures? How does a human being move from an unavailable tweety bird to a lethal rampage? How do a series of persons switch from dejected outcasts to maniacal killers? When we look to our chronicles of horror, we see that the answers to such questions are intricately bound up with panic and with the starkest of existential outlooks. We can surmise, based both on these chronicles and what we know from depth psychology, that each of the above perpetrators has been shattered in some way. Each, for a complex knot of reasons, has been imbued with cosmic meaninglessness. Each is compelled, transfixed, riveted by one overarching theme—his or her crumbling core and the headlong drive to deny it, regardless of costs.

Given the right mix of circumstances, Toby could well go the way of the above youths. I would argue that any of us, given similar circumstances, could, and the bloodbath of the last century is a resounding illustration.

But there is another side to this monster (and indeed human) tale, and it too must be recognized. This is the side of fascination. We can't simply decry the excesses of monstrous acts without recognizing their strange and ironic allure. Without acknowledging the curiosity, charge, or even excitement aroused by physical and emotional excesses, we fail to understand their healing, creative, and developmental potential.

The problem of extremism (monstrosity, fanaticism) is the problem of attachment. Attachment, as philosophers of the East have long pointed out, is truly a problem of overreaching—of grasping after that which eludes or freezing that which flows. The issue, however, is more complicated for not only does attachment frustrate and court monstrosity, it also opens worlds, pushes frontiers, and unveils possibilities—it transports.

"The poetry of transgression," Susan Sontag wrote, "is also knowledge. He who transgresses not only breaks a rule. He goes somewhere that others are not; and he knows something that others don't know."[20] In this context, it is not difficult to see why monstrosity compels us so and why we are enthralled by the Phantom and entranced by Dracula. In the opening chapter of

Frankenstein, sea-faring adventurer Robert Walton encounters a disheveled, weather-beaten man—Victor Frankenstein. Walton interrogates this visitor, who in turn issues the following warning to Walton:

> I do not know that the relation of my disasters will be useful to you; yet when I reflect that you are pursuing the same course, exposing yourself to the same dangers which have rendered me what I am, I imagine that you may deduce an apt moral from my tale, one that may direct you if you succeed in your under-taking and console you in case of failure.[21]

Now this passage engages on several levels. My chief concern, however, is what captivates us about this passage? What is it about the passage that lures us in and propels us into the balance of the book? While many features of the passage may stand out—its adventurous tone, its allusion to morality and so on—I do not believe that these are its primary allures. The chief allure, by contrast, links directly to Frankenstein's employment of the term "disaster." People don't clamor to read or view *Frankenstein* because it helps them to lead cautious lives. They flock to it because it is dangerous; it thrills and reminds them of the vibrance that their own lives lack.

Most of us at some level relish the uncontrolled. We yearn (though not without ambivalence) to witness the monstrous, the freakish, and the alien. In Rudolf Otto's[22] terms we are entranced by the dreadful precisely because it is excessive—precisely because it energizes, unshackles, and at some point enchants. As previously hinted, Frankenstein's tale of grave-digging and experimentation transports us. His creation ensnares us with its size, its power, and its resiliency. Even its deformities—yellowed skin, scarred face, ill-fitting hands—are both captivating and exotic. They take us out of our humdrum lives, and link us with a wider terrain. Like the universe itself, this terrain defies containment, predictability, and composure. It conjures up the awesome, the diverse, and the mutable.

Our enchantment with the macabre can be seen on many levels of juvenile and adult life. The appeal of drama, of life at the physical or emotional edge, is a reflection of this enchantment. Monstrosity is but a pointer, a disturbing and far-sided mirror to more mundane forms of adventurism. Through the mirror of monstrosity, we can see the appeal of fun houses, roller coasters, and dare-devilry. We can understand the mixture of delight and terror in taking experiences to their limit. But it must also be understood that there is a difference between approaching or playing with monstrosity and becoming monstrous. Witnessing Hannibal Lecter (of *Silence of the Lambs*) devour his twentieth victim is very different from being Hannibal Lecter—or Jeffrey Dahmer, for that matter. Roller coasters come to a stop, the carnival ends at nightfall, romantic swoons fade. Monstrosities on the other hand do not relent—at least not in mortal terms; they are unchainable, ungraspable, and unstoppable. Their woundedness and desperation make them licentious but in the most startling way.

Conversely, there is a complex line between dynamic living and monstrosity and it should not be casually drawn. Is passion for knowledge monstrous? Is devotion to work or an idea demonic? When does genius cross over into madness? Poe demurs: "The question is not yet settled whether madness is or is not the loftiest intelligence—whether much that is glorious—whether all that is profound—does not spring from disease of thought."[23]

For me the issue hinges on the question of compulsion. To what degree can one *choose* to pursue knowledge? To what extent can one *diverge* from one's work, idea, etc.? Compulsion implies desperation; desperation yields panic. While it is true that a modicum of such desperation accompanies most noteworthy achievements (e.g., Beethoven's Ninth Symphony, the American Revolution), the question is how that desperation is handled and to what ends? The more I've reflected on this question, the more I've been forced to admit that blind drivenness may well take one beyond the perimeters of deliberative choice; and that choice, in fact, can have a restraining effect on passion. For example, to the degree that one can choose a response to woundedness, one is forced to pause, reflect, and distill. To the degree that one is mastered by one's wound, on the other hand, one is ablaze with reactivity. One becomes mortified and will resort to the most extreme measures to transcend one's self.

This is not to say that choice is invariably pacifying, constricting, or devitalizing—quite the contrary, choice can just as often be intimate, emotionally charged, and spirited. We can "feel" into our decisions as readily as we can plot them out. However, what I am saying is that within their admittedly narrow sphere—their sphere of fixation—the desperate can mobilize far more energy and generate far more activity than those who are centered and deliberate. Consider, for example, the religious and artistic geniuses in history as compared with their conventional peers; or the war heroes—as well as criminals—compared to the marching masses.[24]

The question then is as follows: How can the energizing elements of desperation be optimized by choice? Or to put it more concretely: How can the zeal of desperation seed the calm of deliberation?

Witnesses to Wounding

Survey the topography of American lives and, as suggested previously, two themes ring clear. The first of these is that, for many in our culture, the spiral of development is compact. The hub (or center point) is often a tightly wound knot around which a few lackluster tasks, hollow conversation, and the television are constellated. The (radial) work and play sites—although diversionary—also tend to be constrained. Work consists of a ten or twenty mile drive to a service or commercial outlet in which repeated and laborious duties are performed in a resigned and obligatory manner. Predictably, people utter the same dispiriting words, to the same dispiriting customers, who have been conditioned to desire the same dispiriting products. Afterward, our typical person drives back home at the end of the day, only to engage in the same encumbering motions as he or she enacted a day earlier, and so on. There are of course variations in these patterns, but they are exceptional. For example, a person may "swing" out to a distant relative, or even try out some new culinary, religious, or drug experience, but seldomly is this divergence challenging, deep, or restorative. Rather, it almost invariably echoes the trappings of one's accustomed life—the familiar, the fashionable, or the expedient. In short, many in our society navigate within a shrunken sphere; rarely do they stray from home and when they do stray it is almost entirely encapsulated, contrived, or vicarious.

The children who grow up in such households, moreover, also tend to be imbued with these patterns. They, too, learn to circumvent.

The second overarching theme is that there is scant room for soul-searching in our culture; crises are relegated to the "inconvenient." Suffering? In pain? Get over them in six sessions; seek out the nearest pharmacy; devour the handiest self-help book. While our society has never really prioritized explorations of pain, today the atmosphere is even less conducive to such exploration. As I have suggested, time alone is a diminishing commodity. Along with the declining contexts for substantive reflections about pain, I would argue that the people who had formerly ministered within these contexts are also dwindling. Where are the life-philosophers today? Where are the thinkers, elders, and the caretakers of myth? How does a culture foster mentors, healers, artists of life, in pressure-packed cubicles? Art, as Abe Maslow put it movingly, is one of the few disciplines that prizes the processes of production as much as it does the products themselves.[25] To what extent can a mass market economy promote art—or foster mentors who can foster artists?

Let us be clear then: If we are to move beyond Huxley's "brave new world," if we are to transcend button pushing and a thoroughly regimented lifestyle, then we must alter the socioeconomic map. We must recognize that the capacity to tolerate ambiguity, discord, and, strife is one of the hallmarks of maturation and that without such a reserve, there is almost no chance to thrive. In the research on resilient trauma survivors, two themes consistently emerge. One, the survivors encountered what Alice

Miller termed "helpful witnesses"—mentors, nurturers, parental surrogates—who were integral to survivors' healing. Two, these witnesses helped survivors not just to bear but to constructively transform their misery.[26]

From my vantage point, witnesses in the above scenarios provided a kind of mirroring function to survivors, without which survivors would have been lost. The mirroring function refers to witnesses' capacity to relate personally to survivors' ordeals. Witnesses have "been there," so to speak. They have faced in some substantive measure what the survivors face currently, and they have developed the tools—most probably by being mentored themselves—to contain, translate, and convert incendiary material. Helpful witnesses, thereby, are able to stand firmly by struggling survivors. They are able to ministrate to survivors' wounds, be they physical or emotional. Screams do not topple them, vitriol does not sweep them aside, nor do unabating sadnesses, silences, and withdrawals. Indeed, witnesses preside at everything short of physical attack by survivors, and even in those cases witnesses may be able to promote a restoration.

Through such presence, then, survivors are opened to new and previously unavailable portals through which to view their struggles. They are provided the time, safety, and, stability to identify their battles, explore their bases, and draw upon them to forge new lives. Through witnesses' successes, moreover, survivors also are emboldened to succeed and to transform discordant spirits. Consider, for example, the processes through which such luminaries as Nietzsche and Picasso evolved and thus transcended great odds.[27]

The holding of paradox therefore is a cardinal feature of the healing witness.[28] How many times have such witnesses been called "quirky," "colorful," or "different from the pack?" These attributions speak directly to the contrarieties that witnesses harbor. Witnesses can be both wide-eyed and disciplined, child-like and mature. (To this extent, they strongly resemble the profile of Maslow's self-actualizers and Csikszentmihalyi's creative types).[29] They can act like rowdy teenagers, and yet they can engage in the most sophisticated and high-level activities (e.g., music, writing, and teaching). They tend to find their own paths in life and to associate with others who have also bucked the tide. At the same time, they are not averse to being formal, diplomatic, and even conventional from time to time as the occasion demands. Such people are seasoned veterans of life. They have borne witness to many of life's sorrows and they have taken their own share of falls, false turns, and humiliating jabs. But they have not become mired in these mishaps; they have also partaken in joyous personal or collective breakthroughs, spiritual awakenings, and creative transformations. They are risk-takers who open to both the glories and costs of such practices, and they inspire others to also take risks and experience the range of their possibilities.

As previously suggested, there is something about questing for the whole of life that steeps witnesses in their own and others' many-sidedness and contradictoriness. These qualities exist in many people, to be sure, but they are especially salient in the self-aware.[30]

While witnesses are often living people, this is not necessarily so. Goethe, for example, was a sublime inspiration—even decades after his death. In the moving passage to follow, Nietzsche punctuates this sentiment:

> Goethe sought help from history, natural science, antiquity, and also Spinoza, but above all, from practical activity; he surrounded himself with limited horizons; he did not retire from life but put himself into the midst of it; he was not fainthearted but took as much as possible upon himself, over himself, into himself. What he wanted was *totality*; he fought extraneousness of reason, senses, feeling, and will.... he disciplined himself to wholeness, he *created* himself....
>
> Goethe conceived a human being who would be strong, highly educated, skillful in all bodily matters, self-controlled, reverent toward himself, and who might dare to afford the whole range and wealth of being natural, being strong enough for such freedom; the man of tolerance, not from weakness but from strength.... Such a spirit who has *become free* stands amid

the cosmos with a joyous fatalism, in the *faith* that only the particular is loathsome, and all is redeemed in the whole.[31]

Toby's helpful witness was Uncle Jack. Uncle Jack lived in the rural pastures of Ohio, two hours away from Toby's urban home.

Uncle Jack had an intriguing past. He was a sixtyish ex-postal clerk who was educated as an attorney. Legend has it that Uncle Jack made it all the way to the bar exam, but declined to complete it. Frequently picked on as a child, Uncle Jack was the youngest of three siblings. He was constantly chided for his slight stature, his intellect, and his thoughtful demeanor. His brothers teased him mercilessly, and his parents were either stern or indifferent toward him. The only warmth that Uncle Jack could muster growing up was through friends and books.

Uncle Jack emerged at a timely point in Toby's life. Still devastated by the death of his father, the withdrawal and bitterness of his mother, and the isolation of being a single child, Toby was sinking ever deeper into depression. Sensing Toby's torment, Uncle Jack made increasing contact with him. Sometimes he would seek Toby out and other times Toby and his mother sought his presence. Even Toby's mother recognized the value of Uncle Jack's engagement with Toby, and others could observe it as well.

Uncle Jack was a kindly man with a craggy and distinctive face. He was humorous, playful, and perceptive. He knew how to invite and sometimes gently challenge Toby to try out new experiences, but he also sensed when to pull back and enable Toby to work out issues himself. There was a constant feeling about Uncle Jack that he had really lived. Sometimes that living was resilient and triumphal—for example, he was a quite good artist, having painted many pastoral scenes on his diverse travels throughout the world. At other times, however, Uncle Jack was a frightened, self-absorbed child. He refrained from becoming a lawyer, for example, not only in rebellion against a constricting conventional lifestyle, but also because he was terrified of tradition, authority, and structure. He loved women, but he was reluctant to commit to them, or to start a family. Yet Uncle Jack evolved throughout his life.

While he never became a lawyer or married, he did learn to assert, commit, and deepen himself in other ways. By the time he entered Toby's life, he was an accomplished (if not acclaimed) painter, a seasoned traveler, and a beloved civic activist. Further, he lived his life with integrity, consistently upholding the values he believed in, and reflective about those with which he disagreed.

For Toby, one of the most important features of Uncle Jack's life was his home. That home was a veritable treasure-trove—chock full of travel mementos, anthropological finds, games, sports equipment, and classical books. Echoing his Renaissance life, Uncle Jack's residence was vibrant, stately, and mysterious. The place was a real "find" for Uncle Jack, who, between a modest inheritance and a pension, was able to live on a one-acre lot, adjacent to running brooks and thick woods. For Toby, the contrast between his own and Uncle Jack's place could not be starker. Whereas Toby lived in a small urban box house, his Uncle's residence was spacious, turn-of-the-century, and rural; and whereas Toby's house was spare and austere, Uncle Jack's was brimming with warmth and character. One of Toby's favorite pastimes was to visit Uncle Jack at Halloween. The colors of the countryside were brilliant at this time, and so were Uncle Jack's meticulous arrangements. Uncle Jack had a deep sense about Halloween and he elevated it to a fine art. Every Halloween eve, he would adorn his home with orange and black candles, hang an assortment of strategically placed creatures, and prepare a macabre and fascinating ceremony in his basement. Halloween day would begin with Toby, Uncle Jack, and a pack of neighborhood kids carving pumpkins. Uncle Jack would crack jokes with the children, show them a variety of pumpkin-carving techniques, and lead them on a ghost hunt throughout his carefully arranged amusements. Next, he would assist the kids to put on a play, such as *The Wizard of Oz* or one they made up themselves, and perform this play before parents and other children in the neighborhood. By the time evening fell, Uncle Jack would invite about ten children into his basement for "mystery readings." These readings consisted of some of the scariest short stories in "All Hallows Eve" lore. In the festive and dimly lit basement, the children would be assembled in a circle and one by one would read a passage from one of the stories. When appropriate, Uncle Jack would provide creative and entertaining sound effects, visual displays, and surprise guests. One year Uncle Jack's neighbor, Jim, showed up as a cape-clad Phantom playing a church organ.

For Toby, Uncle Jack's Halloween and other such occasions provided just the salve for his burdened heart. Toby had been estranged, forlorn, and spiritually depleted. His mother made valiant efforts to address these maladies, but was too depleted herself—too enmeshed in scraping out a living, too embittered by the past—to substantively help. What Uncle Jack offered, on the other hand, was a world away from these spiraling torments. He offered a refuge, a place of fun and mystery, discovery and support, that energized Toby, and provided new impetus for him to play, learn, and mobilize his resources. Uncle Jack was able to "hold" Toby (similar to the way good therapists "hold" their clients) and enable him to see his hurts—such as his sense of estrangement, for example—in new ways. Toby began to see that feeling lost and alone was not a wholly uncommon experience, that others (such as Uncle Jack himself) had also undergone such trials, and that those experiences can be survived. Further, Uncle Jack helped him to see that such difficulties could connect people with something fresh, enlivening, and even potentially thrilling, if they could but stay present to them. Given his blend of quirkiness and stability, playfulness and earnestness, and fine-grained empathy along with leathery toughness, Uncle Jack helped Toby to see that conflict and contradiction can coexist simultaneously, and, indeed, fruitfully within one soul.

Like Pablo in Hermann Hesse's *Steppenwolf*, Uncle Jack led Toby through a "magic theater." This theater was labyrinthine, had many unsettling passages, and sometimes perturbed Toby, but it brimmed with life—as against the "death" that Toby experienced at home. In essence the theater awakened Toby to his larger self—the self that is inspired by choice, imagination, and love. It is a self that holds poignancy alongside loneliness; meditation alongside forlornness; and fiery passion alongside rage.

Grapplers with Groundlessness

Uncle Jack's salutary impact on Toby is attributable to many factors—his caring and concern for Toby, his attendance to the boy's
despair, Toby's own (inner and outer) resources, and so on. However, the chief point I wish to make here is that beyond all the conventional understanding of Uncle Jack's influence on Toby, there
is an influence of a much subtler, weightier kind. Specifically, this
influence is reflected in Uncle Jack's appreciation of the scope of
Toby's struggle. Let me explain.

Uncle Jack's sensitivity to Toby went beyond Toby's bereavement over the death of his father, but to the implications of that
bereavement for Toby's entire world-design. Recognizing that Toby's pain was far from circumscribed, Uncle Jack saw that it had
enormous intrapersonal and interpersonal reverberations. Uncle
Jack further intuited that Toby's bereavement was connected to
profound existential anxieties—the separation from comforting
ideals, the wrenching from security, and the shattering of hopes.
Although Uncle Jack may not have explicitly understood these
"stakes" in Toby's ordeal, he did sense them symbolically, based on
his own life experience. Like the best witnesses, in my view, Uncle
Jack recognized a cosmic dimension to Toby's battle. He saw that
losing a father (or mother or any close relationship) means losing
a part of one's world. By implication, it means discovering oneself
"shipwrecked" on a new world, a further horizon. This discovery,
in turn, anticipates even further worlds and horizons, with even
further catastrophic possibilities. Such is the nature of subliminal
processing—once the disturbing content is identified, it abruptly
forms linkages with similar contents, the implications of which
conjure yet further echoes of disturbance. This indefinite regress,
moreover, is not merely representative of cognitive distortion, but
is a central feature of our subliminal lives. As careful students of
psyche have suggested, the subconscious sectors of our experience may be as illuminating as they are stupefying. Anxieties
about death, decay, illness and the like may be "irrational" from
one standpoint; but from another standpoint, they are supremely

astute—for such forces beset us all the time, shade our everyday concerns, and impact us palpably, no matter how stable our circumstances. Similarly, as suggested earlier, children's fears of the dark, of wind, and of monsters are not so amiss in this quagmire within which we live. Who but for the most callous would fail to grant this aforementioned problem, or the obliqueness toward which we are thrust. In short, subconscious regions of self embrace a vast neural and sensory network. Among the by-products of this network are fantasies, projections, and exaggerations, as well as stark realizations about life.

"If the doors of perception were cleansed," wrote William Blake, "everything would appear as it is to man, infinite."[32]

The best witnesses have polished, if not cleansed, the doors of perception. Witnesses like Uncle Jack have absorbed the foundation-shaking and metaphysical into their lives. They have taken up their own and others' smallness, insignificance, and even nothingness into their life-philosophies. They have heeded the Taoist lesson that we have little ultimate control, that we are vastly overpowered, and that appreciation, reflection, and discernment betoken wisdom. They have also absorbed the lesson of the temporal—that emotions and fixations pass, that all life evolves, and that change is inevitable. This attitude of engaged nonattachment is associated with a generous approach to self, others, and life itself. It is an approach that helped Toby, for example, when he flew into tantrums or tapped panic. Through Uncle Jack's patience, tolerance, and anticipation of change, Toby was able to view his "episodes" with less drama and a wider vision and thereby became less needful of them.

At the same time that witnesses such as Uncle Jack acknowledge their smallness, however, they also (and by implication) discover their greatness and their capacity to overcome their dire plights. Through their comparative attunement to things, in other words, witnesses learn much about what can and cannot be altered. They learn about the passing nature of fear, for example, and the recuperation of strength, but they also learn about the periodic pain that is requisite to bear those experiences.

Above all, perhaps, witnesses learn to choose their battles, prioritize, and channel their intensive energy. Through quiet reflection, they are able to clarify that which is substantively demanded of them, and the will or spirit to address that which is demanded. For example, through the plethora of talks, walks, and provisions of solitude, Uncle Jack helped Toby to find his strength, and Toby, in turn, was able to take more risks with Uncle Jack, to forgo many of his anxieties, and to participate in the vibrancy of Uncle Jack's household.

What would the world look like if more caretakers had Uncle Jack's sense of infinity? What if *society* were an optimal witness? How would children of all walks of life develop? These are bold but necessary questions. If we are to take the helpful witness concept seriously, if we are to look closely at the trajectories of resilient lives, then we must acknowledge the implications they raise, not only for the development of individuals and families, but also for society as a whole and for social philosophies as a whole.

Does Vivacity Require Trauma?

As we survey the landscape of awe-filled and dynamic lives, one of the first issues to strike us is this population's travails. Uncle Jack was severely demeaned, Toby was abandoned; many other creative and resilient types are abused, neglected, and infirmed.[33] While there does seem to be a preponderance of such affliction associated with invigorating lives, a very puzzling dilemma arises—do people have to suffer to develop extraordinary abilities? Put another way, is trauma a prerequisite for exceptional health? Moreover, if trauma is a prerequisite for maximal well-being, then very unsettling questions need to be asked about how to promote such a linkage. Do we need (in some sense) to "create" traumatic conditions? Would the latter be used to justify harsh or abrasive treatment—warfare, abuse, insults?

After much reflection, I have come to the conclusion that the above conundrums are partially if not wholly avoidable. First, while there are many compelling sides to the trauma/health proposition, I do not think it addresses the larger picture. Some people, for example, become extraordinary examples of health and resilience, yet do not arise from turbulent backgrounds. Consider, for example, the relatively pacific life of Johann Sebastian Bach.[34] How do these people achieve their successes? Second, biology, temperament, and cultural context, also surely play some role in the advent of well being.

The bigger picture, therefore, seems to entail more than trauma, but acuity of perception. It's not so much that one has to be traumatized to become hardy, but that for the latter to unfold, one has to achieve the equivalency of traumatic illumination. How does one achieve this equivalency? The only way of which I am aware is to develop a sensitivity to the ordinary challenges of living—illness, separation, loss—and to find ways to constructively transform this sensitivity. Developmentally speaking, this contention brings us back to the necessity for engaged caretaking, not merely for the overtly wounded, but also for the populace of woundedness as a whole. Uncle Jack is an example par excellence of a witness who ministers to youth, not just to the Tobys of the world. He is the kind of conscious renegade who challenges youth to live passionate, engaged lives. He challenges youth to venerate, to quiver, to thrill, and to doubt before the spectacle of existence. In full recognition that the skull grins at the banquet and that death inheres in life, he also sees the poignancy to this ever-looming dilemma, the exhilarating opportunities it presents. The task that Uncle Jack sets, then, is to fashion something out of these opportunities, to offer something of value.[35]

The point of Uncle Jack's teaching can be summarized as follows: Every day there is an opportunity for awe. In every person, there is fear, struggle, and exuberance, and at every moment, there is an opportunity to transform.

The question for Toby—and equally importantly, for the world—is how much benefit does such a transformation offer? How much does it enliven, energize, or inspirit? For Toby, the answer is stark: He was emboldened to thrive under Uncle Jack's tutelage and, through his own restoration, to embolden others.

For the world, however, the answer is much less defined. Traditionally, the question of transformation has been relegated to the major world religions—and more recently, to political and psychotherapeutic arenas—and yet these institutions bespeak a very mixed record. To be sure, there are segments of the aforementioned that appear to be more elevating than other portions, and each institution has provided sustenance for many. But numerous problems arise about this sustenance—whom does it benefit, under which conditions, and at what personal or social cost?

Institutions have a curious legacy on our planet. On one hand they have eased the suffering—both physical and spiritual—of millions; on the other, they have divided, enraged, and devitalized. Almost without exception, it seems, every country that has embraced the major religious and secular institutions of our time has been—and continues to be—tainted. They are bullied by dictatorships, oligarchies, and theocracies, or they are wracked by bigotry, feuds, and war. While each must search his or her own soul to determine the corrective to these predicaments, we humans—as both nations and as individuals—can do significantly better. My conclusion is that conventional remedies for life's trials tend to be either stopgap palliatives at best, or rapid descents into self-destruction at worst. The chief problem is that few institutions ask the starker questions about life—who are we, what are we, and where are we all headed? It is rare, for example, to find a conventionally religious Uncle Jack, or a dogmatic helpful witness. Conversely, it is equally rare to find clergy who openly acknowledge life's paradoxes: the anxieties beneath the most composed appearances, the impotencies within the most heralded authorities and the love, faith, or generosities of the most freethinking dissenters.

"For life is at the start a chaos," José Ortega y Gasset reminds us, but I prefer to take my cue from German theologian Rudolf Otto, for whom life is at the start a tremendous mystery (*mysterium tremendum*).[36] It is a shaking, quaking, dread-inducing affair, an experience of abject fragility before creation. But at the same time, as Otto insists, it is also an amazing affair. Arising from our fundamental experience of *mysterium,* he observes, is the equally intensive experience of enthrallment, inspiration, and fascination. Not only do we feel apart from creation, we also feel a part of it—swept up by it, enjoined to it, and enlarged through its magnitude.

The problem is that few are willing to face this ambiguous plight. Few are willing to acknowledge both their smallness, humbleness before creation, as well as their boldness and capacity for adventure. This is our awe-deprived condition today, and it is a product not just of institutional life, but, increasingly, of the life of individuals as well. We in the industrialized world are increasingly immune to awe—even in our homes, on our walks, or with our lovers. Ironically, even the meager awe we do experience—as illustrated by highly focused fears, passing or vicarious thrills, and corrosive worries—are all but on the brink of eradication as well. Aided by television, media blitzes, and designer drugs, we have less and less need to grapple with ourselves, to probe into our concerns, or to sift through our multifaceted emotions. We now have drugs, for example, that not only radically alter moods, but also sex drives and memories. Troubled by the trials of youth? Take a memory "eraser." Aggravated by an unfulfilled marriage? Ingest Viagra. Blue over a corporate merger? Pop a Zoloft. Soon we will have drugs that will prevent or forestall disabilities, deformations, and dysfunctions of almost any kind. Want "perfection" in the next generation? Take a DNA enhancer. We have hundreds of cable channels, millions of websites. Disturbed by childhood violence? Distract yourself with game shows, "reality" TV, and sports networks.

In short, the path of least resistance is the new societal watchword, and the atrophy of passion is its price.

Yet we must not conclude too hastily on these matters. There are useful, even magical, aspects to our contemporary environment. As cosmetic as certain mood altering drugs may be, for example, to some folks they are life-saving. Information technology may be devitalizing in many circumstances, but in emergencies it is critical.

On the other side of the coin, there are ironies aplenty about dynamic and creative people. Not only, as previously noted, do such people tend to suffer as youth, but they also tend to live stormily as adults. Nietzsche, for example, became a brilliant philosopher of liberation, but to women he was something of an ogre. Picasso blazed inimical artistic trails, but to many who knew him, he was a lout. R.D. Laing displayed unprecedented acuity when it came to his psychotic patients, but in his personal life, he could be boorish, reckless, and violent.[37] And the list goes on.

The risks of a fluid center, then, are formidable. Those who stretch limits, who passionately tangle with life, are also sometimes casualties of those endeavors. Their heroism and nobility in one area may be cruelly countered in another. But the eternal question remains. Is it better to have lived and lost than not to have lived at all? My answer is as resounding as the lives I have illustrated. There is no substitute for a fully engaged life. To be sure, many innovators founder at times, they make public spectacles of themselves, but on balance their service has far outweighed their disservice, and their inspiration to others is measureless.[38]

The value of the celebrated—and even relatively anonymous—actualizer, if we may borrow that term, is that she or he points to a virtually forgotten component of psychological maturation. Beyond skill acquisition and cultural competency, beyond even the capacity to form empathic bonds, is the foundational attunement to awe. Awe is the developmental soup; skills, competencies, and the like are the garnish. Without awe, skills and competencies pale, empathy withers. There are many people who function superbly at their jobs or social roles, but their sense of passion, commitment, and vision correlates directly with their capacity for awe. Likewise, there are many people who tolerate others but who lack the genuine capacity to be open to others, which is contingent on awe.[39]

The sense of awe, as suggested earlier, is probably inherent to life. A child's first memories are both thrilling and humbling, amazing and overwhelming. There is so much to learn about one's caretakers, one's surroundings, and one's movements. The question is what happens to that awe, how does it erode, and go dim? Take the simple subject of colors. Why are they so mesmerizing to pre-schoolers? My son sees a green crayon and he's overjoyed. "Greeeeen!" he exclaims upon seeing the corresponding implement. What is it about fairy tales, monsters, and super-heroes? Every little boy I knew as a kid loved adventure tales—*Treasure Island, Swiss Family Robinson, Huckleberry Finn*. My own son loves Pokemon, Batman, and Zorro. And many girls are not exempt from similar fancies with their exuberance over Dorothy in *The Wizard of Oz*, Wonder Woman, and Xena. These characters, it seems to me, are touchstones for awe, for the unquenchable thirst for discovery—they fly, they leap, and they evolve. Like children, they cavort with the primal—earth, sky, sea, and storm. They evoke the range of feelings about life—its fragility and its power, its mystery and its pageantry. They also help children to manage these primal realities. Consider the recent craze over the Harry Potter serials!

The questions and curiosities of the young, therefore, are renown. But what of the adult environments they typically enter— the depressions, cynicisms, and conformities, the frustrations, hostilities, and insensitivities? Are these arenas not awe-depleting, physically stunting, and intellectually impoverishing. How different our world would be if awe became as commonplace as competency in our culture. How different our children would be. Lest I be misunderstood, here, I am not arguing against the need for some measure of structure or even competency in child development—indeed, as I suggested earlier, awe does not preclude them. But what I am arguing for is proportionality regarding the latter, a means of redress.

What would it be like then if children the world over could adopt an Uncle Jack? What if their cries for discovery and play were met with the same zest and verve?

What if colors became something that parents too could embrace—allowing green, for example, to echo in their emotions, imaginations, or reminiscences? What if parents reveled in their children's physicality—running, dancing, or rolling along with them, or permitted themselves to sing and to make up silly words with their children, or to relish toy stores or natural history museums, or to wonder at super heroes or great beasts? What if parents showed their children the stars or talked with them about dreams, or if they spent time to respond to children's curiosities or to acknowledge their anxieties? What if parents could resonate with their entire bodies when children hugged them or sang songs or simply talked? What if they could really "take in" their time with their children, and not just in pleasant times but in sad, angry, or even hurt times as well? How different it would be to admonish a child within a context of warmth and wonder as opposed to terseness and animosity, and how refreshing to marvel at a child's playroom or the clutter strewn about the floor.

But these fine sentiments are moot if parents cannot experience awe, if they cannot access awe. And how can they access awe if it is so muted today—physically, emotionally, and intellectually? These are issues to which we will momentarily turn and attempt to answer.

Summary of the Fluid Center Developmental Position

In the preceding section, I have attempted to restore the vibrancy, pathos, and awe that grounds living developmental psychology. Far from being exhaustive, this endeavor is but a beginning, a shot across the bow, if you will, to remind psychology of its calling. The fluid center developmental position can be summarized as follows: Consciousness begins with gestation, delivery, and birth. The earliest signs of consciousness cluster around the sense of centeredness (constraint, containment) and fluidity (extension, movement). As development proceeds, the capacity for both centeredness and fluidity are enhanced. The child becomes more centered, for example, through increasing abilities to channel, delay, and structure her impulses. She becomes more fluid through growing abilities to explore, express, and experiment with her impulses.

At the core of these abilities is the child's sense of awe—the thrill and anxiety before being. The child is thrilled, for example, at her comfortable surroundings, at her capacity to move and to play in these surroundings, and at her growing capacity to influence her surroundings. She is also thrilled, at least to a point, by the uncontrollable in her environment—climate, people, animals, changes in patterns, colors, and textures. These very same experiences however, can turn disturbing. The thrill of centeredness, for example, can become the anxiety of constraint; the excitation of fluidity, on the other hand, can become the dread of unruliness. Depending on how the child negotiates these twin poles of awe—her centeredness and fluidity before being—her trajectory of development is established.[40]

The trajectory of development is dependent on many factors—the child's temperament, her caretaker's response to the temperament, her immediate environment, biological and circumstantial eventualities, and so on. The problem is that traditional developmental psychology focuses on the normative dimensions of this trajectory—adjustment to or deviation from cultural standards, cognitive and behavioral "competencies," and emotional moderation. But these traditional foci have only illuminated a very restrictive range of human capability (that which I term "encapsulated fluidity"), and they have proven inept in understanding the crux of human capability—the unfolding and elaboration of awe. Due precisely to this omission, there is an almost wholesale failure among conventional theorists to grasp the heights as well as depths of developmental processes. For example, suffering and dysfunction are reduced to pathologies. Pathologies are discretely observable and measurable deviations from the norm. Health, healing, and growth, on the other hand, are reduced to observable and measurable adjustments to the norm. Taken together, conventional theorizing addresses highly circumscribed spheres of human transformation—physiological, behavioral, cognitive, psychosexual, and interpersonal deviations from and approximations to the norm, but the stakes are much higher. The implications of human struggle, of suffering, and of health and healing are foundation-shaking. They relate to self, family, and culture, to be sure, but they also relate to being, to the fathomless borders of creation.

In my formulation of this problem, I showed that being affects development in two basic ways—by overwhelming and thereby polarizing, or by beckoning and thereby enlarging experiential outlooks. The degree to which being polarizes or beckons hinges greatly on the trajectory of one's development. If one's development warps in the direction of cosmic insignificance, one tends to inflate oneself and hyperexpand to overcompensate. If, on the other hand, one's development warps in the direction of cosmic disarray, one tends to deflate oneself and become hyperconstrictive to cope. In Western society, people often experience both polarities in varying degrees and react or hyperreact accordingly. However, the conventional developmental stance in our world is neither deflated nor grandiose, neither groveling nor lavish, but static, blunted, and removed.

The story of Toby and Jack points to yet a fourth developmental alternative. Toby was neither stuck in polarization nor lulled by superficiality. Through his trauma and, equally important, Jack's tutelage, Toby discovered a further horizon—vitality. By staying present to his torments, Toby was able to learn from and transform them. Through loss, depression, and rage, he was able to cultivate new capacities for solitude, reflection, and passion.

The chief question of this chapter is whether or not people of diverse backgrounds can optimize openness, fluidity, and range, as well as containment, centeredness, and focus. Can a whole society acknowledge this wormlike/birdlike condition; and the palpable travail-yet-verve to which it is linked? I believe so, but it will only happen with activism and the patience to "plant seeds."

PART II:

Visions of Recovery: Social,
Vocational, and Educational

3

Toward a Social Fluid Center

And who knows (there is no saying with certainty), perhaps the only goal on earth to which mankind is striving lies in this incessant process of attaining, in other words, in life itself, and not the thing to be attained, which must always be expressed as a formula, as positive as twice two makes four, [yet] such positiveness is not life, gentlemen, [it] is the beginning of death.

—Fyodor Dostoyevsky (*Notes from underground*, 1864)[1]

It is a fundamental principle of living that wherever consciousness fixates, it simultaneously deviates. We can deny this tendency, but our dreams, displacements, and physiology will almost invariably betray us.

Even when consciousness is proclaimed to be all-pervading, it finds a way to rebel. If I am told that I am godlike, for example, I almost invariably experience an accompanying twinge of wormlikeness; anxiety and unsettlement become palpable. If I am immortalized, I instantly feel a pang of mortality; at some level, I yearn for confinement, tradition, security. Am I a neurotic mess? I think not. I believe that most people, and quite possibly everyone (in their inmost being), share my oscillations. Not just the mind but also the heart cries out to diverge. Consider the lover, for example, who pines for solitude, the vagabond who yearns for stability, and the thinker who hungers for sentiment.

Many treatises and spiritual teachings have been premised on human ambivalence. "Knowledge," as Hermann Hesse suggests in his eloquent novella on Buddhism, is a one-sided affair; wisdom is paradoxical. "In every truth the opposite is equally true."[2] The world today is full of "learning," full of information about this or that subject, but very short on wisdom. To be wise about our social and vocational lives requires a profound reorientation (literally, a rearrangement of our stance). We need to discover, like Toby, that beliefs, assurances, and perceptions contain their own contraries, and that wisdom derives from sorting out these contraries, filtering them through, and risking a decision in spite (and in light) of them.

To recognize life's paradoxes is to perceive its awe.

Freud too sniffed out the profundity of paradox. "The mind," he suggests, "is...a sort of tumbling-ground for the struggles of antagonistic impulses.... To express it in non-dynamic terms," he goes on, "the mind is made up of contradictions and pairs of opposites."[3]

As theorists from Eliade to Levi-Strauss have shown, most cultures acknowledge human paradoxes. Freedom and limitation, individuality and society, and sacredness and profanity are integral to communal life. However, how many cultures and cultural paradigms explore the intricacies out of which such paradoxes emerge?

Many—particularly in consumerist cultures—view people as simpletons. The pretense is that how people act outwardly or what they convey verbally is who they are fundamentally. If people say they want a handgun or a strong military or a new Cadillac or a cupboard full of cookies or a 100-channel television or a pocket size computer or an omnipotent savior, then by golly that's what they truly crave and should be given! It is on the basis of this pretense, furthermore, that institutions provide for people, give them pat phrases or ready formulas—and people "buy" these palliatives, not because they believe in them with all their heart and might, but because they yearn for the lie that the palliatives supply; and that lie is conditioned very early on. The lie proceeds as follows: Living is one-dimensional,[4] people seek elemental pleasures, and elemental pleasures are elementally met. Although people must struggle periodically to attain their goals, they are essentially passive, complacent, and hedonistic.

While the latter modalities can be adaptive, to be sure, the question is, are we *reducible* to them; and should a whole society be *founded* on them?[5]

The one-dimensional thinking that people have here-to-date exhibited does not bode well for a vibrant civilization. Wherever it has been deployed, division, polarization, and deprivation have too often resulted. Much of what we call human misery, in fact, can be laid at its "doorstep."

Today, the world is in a very mixed situation. The one-dimensional thinking of free-market capitalism has opened up trade and relations on an unheard-of international scale. The goods and services that have arisen from this ideology have greatly elevated the standard of many people's lives. At the same time, however, it has been associated with an unprecedented split between rich and poor, negligent work conditions, skyrocketing environmental hazards, and alarming rates of depression.[6]

To complicate this picture, increasing numbers of children (the emerging generation) are being weaned on one of the most elemental of palliatives, drugs. In the year 2000, according to the *New York Times* (8/19/01), almost twenty million prescriptions were written for stimulants, "most of them for children," and drug sales reached $758 million.[7] In light of these trends, hard questions must be raised about children's preparedness for life, their tolerance for struggle, their motivation to introspect, and their capacity to transform.

The danger here is palpable. With increasing numbers of one-dimensional people, gratifying one-dimensional needs, there is a mounting specter of breakdown. Elemental fulfillment can only take a society so far; community, self-initiative, and complexity are likely to be its casualties.

As early as 1936, Ortega y Gasset foresaw the peril. Our main danger, he writes, is "inertia." It's not that the masses are evil, Ortega notes, it is that they have become vulgar, apathetic, and, in a word, spoiled. We have entered an era of "radical ingratitude" according to Ortega, and, like the indulged heirs to dynastic rulers, people of today have become bloated, entitled, and smug. There are fewer nobles today, according to Ortega, for nobility "is synonymous with a life of effort" and this life "stands opposed to the common or inert life, which reclines statically upon itself…"[8] It is difficult to participate in the co-creation of one's existence, Ortega elaborates, and to reap the benefits of that evolution, if one is sated from birth and devoid of conflict or want. Quite to the contrary, one feels oneself to be something of an imposter (or "mirrored light") rather than a shaper or fosterer of life. The position, however, is ironic, because at the same time that many experience guilt over their self-imposed idleness, they also, at a more superficial level, experience the inflation of their inheritance. And these two polarities—guilt and entitlement, devaluation and inflation—can wreak havoc, as we have seen in dynastic societies.

The upshot of this digression is that technical proficiency and know-how can produce a comfortable and well-informed citizenry, but only to a point: to the degree that point is crossed, people lose their initiative, their will to explore, and their powers to transform. There must be more to a societal system than the gratification of elemental needs; there must be room for the tacit, the experiential, and the probative. And we must pursue these if we are to pursue life.

What then would the world look like, if it honored the oscillating psyche, if it honored paradox? This is the monumental problem to which we will now turn.

Templates

In the section to follow, I will examine three fluidly centered social paradigms—carnival, awe-based vocation, and awe-based education. While these paradigms are partly hypothetical, they should not be mistaken as illusory. They are as illusory (or concrete) as we choose.

The Spirit of Carnival

Carnival is an archetype: dark yet dazzling—near yet elusive—within the yawning human depths.

Carnival is dark because it puzzles; it is dazzling because it thrills.

The nearness of carnival is palpable. Who among us does not reverberate still to the whirring of roller coasters, the frenzy of fun-houses, and the frolic of dress-up?

Carnivals are elusive, on the other hand, because, for the most part, they belong to a bygone era—our childhoods. Subsequent to our childhoods, it seems, many of us lose the taste, zest, and spirit of unbarred merriment.

Today carnivals have become peripheral. While amusement parks and isolated festivals abound, they are increasingly commercial, compartmentalized, and remote from the cultural fabric. Less and less today do our lives intersect with the native, the imaginative, and the mischievous. By contrast, these have been replaced by the programmed, the canned, and the virtual. Rarely are we encouraged to loosen up in our era—to sing, to dance, and to collectively revel.

Yet carnival is critical to us—it has always been thus. Carnival is one of the rare chances to be something that one is not but paradoxically may potentially be. One of the hallmarks of carnival is the experimental and playful within the relatively safe and contained. Carnival has been called "ordered play." It is a chance to try out the many and contrasting sides of oneself in a community of many and contrasting dimensions.[9]

Carnival arose historically out of the anguish of the powerless and out of the recognition of that anguish by those who mediated their fate. While there have been many forms of powerlessness, and many expressions of carnival, the classic example of such activity for Westerners was feudal Europe.[10] On the whole, life in feudal Europe was onerous. Although elevated to a certain degree by their Christian hopes and rituals, the citizens of feudal Europe were by and large oppressed, devalued, and entrapped. Kings tyrannized the state and priests pulverized the mind. One of the few outlets for the citizenry, however, was the carnival and feast during harvest days. Representing the ancient markings of spring harvest and autumnal culling, carnival provided a major opportunity for merriment, gorging, and celebration of the flesh. Particularly prior to the Christian period of Lent (the weeks preceding Easter), carnival reached a peak of intensity. At these times, there would be exotic parades, inimitable adornments, provocative mask-wearing, and interminable imbibing. There would also be orgiastic sexual practices, enchanting amusements, and incessant vulgarity. Belly-aching humor, mockery, and indulgence were the order of the day. Integral to Lenten carnivals was the connection with and expression of the body. The body represented all that epitomized life—birth and decay, ecstasy and terror, constraint and expanse.[11]

Let us look more closely now at this Lenten prototype, for in its intricacies, we will find the seeds of a revolution.

The Structure of Carnival

Carnival is distinguished by an assemblage of polarities, each reflecting fluidity and centrality. Among the polarities are: limitation and freedom, form and vitality, order and disorder, individuality and collectivity, diversity and unity, degeneration and regeneration, humor and sacredness, and earthiness and spirituality. The beauty of carnival is that it echoes life on so many levels: the mental, the physical, and the metaphysical.

Carnival also evokes and was probably drawn from the cycles of nature—contraction and expansion, death and rebirth, and decay and regeneration.[12] But carnival evokes a great deal more; it elucidates a vision. The vision that carnival suggests is a staging ground, a model, for the embracing of paradox. Through carnival, we not only gain a window on who we are, but we also gain a portal on how we can play with, shape, and animate who we are.

To begin our study of carnival, let us consider a typical carnival scenario. The preparations for carnival begin weeks or even years before the festive event itself. One of the first challenges a reveler faces is how she is to participate—what role she is to play—in the upcoming event. Role-play is a pivotal dimension of

carnival. While some roles are culturally or circumstantially pre-
scribed, generally speaking, one chooses a carnival role because
one is curious about it, or it gives one a chance to tap an unfa-
miliar dimension of oneself. I might want to try out an outlaw
role, for example, because it represents an enticing yet recessed
side of myself. One parallel to this kind of role shifting is the literary phenomenon known as the "doppelganger" (or "double").[13]
Throughout Western literature, the double has served as a portal
to self-discovery, an expanded sense of being. In *Dr. Jekyll and Mr.
Hyde*, for example, a mild-mannered everyman unveils his "wild
man." In *The Portrait of Dorian Gray*, a vain but aging cad revives
(if temporarily) the blush of his youth. In *A Christmas Carol*,
Scrooge discovers his magnanimity. And so on.

What these parables and the carnivalesque share in common
is enlargement, both of self and of world. For example, they both
elaborate the extremes and anxieties of human potential, but they
also do not neglect the zeal, wonder, and vitality that accompany
those extremes and anxieties. They face enlargement "head on,"
as it were.

In the therapy office, we also discover these exhilarating shifts
of living. Healing, from my standpoint, is "self reoccupation." It
is the reoccupation of the parts of oneself that have been cut off
from oneself and the absorption consequently of new and evolving parts. The more that we can reoccupy our selves, moreover,
the more that we can inspire others to reoccupy their selves and,
as a result, share in the dynamism of an enlarged consciousness.
Contrary to popular belief, however, such engagement does not
have to court anarchy. It does not have to eventuate in chaos. In
fact, we know from depth therapy that just the opposite tends to
result—particularly in the absence of panic. Rather than diffus-
ing identity formation, play and experimentation actually tend
to strengthen it, and rather than exacerbating extremes, play and
experimentation actually tend to temper them. The key to such
flourishing, however, is safety. To the degree that play and experimentation can be engaged safely, in contained and supportive
environments, they are likely to be accompanied by discernment,

sensitivity, and responsibility.

This sequence is observed over and over again with clients. The more that clients are able to stay present to themselves—particularly their affective and kinesthetic selves—the more they are able to clarify (and hence prioritize) that which deeply matters. And that which deeply matters tends be much more than idle self-absorption; but also life, love, and community. The analogue to carnival here is not lost. The capacities to play, to explore, and to revel collectively in people's unique creations are precisely carnival's hallmarks; and precisely the tragedy today, in our carnival-deprived age.

Conditions for a Social Fluid Center

What can happiness mean for man, except to realize that life is a gift, and not a burden? And how can modern man convert life from a burden into a gift, except by consecrating it in the service of a self-transcending cause? As Gabriel Marcel has so acutely understood, it is only in this way that life becomes a gift because it becomes something that man can give to meanings and purposes that transcend his own. The individual finite life is intimately linked with ultimate concern. This is why modern man whines so pitifully with the burden of life—he has nothing ultimate to dedicate it to; nothing infinite to assume responsibility for; nothing self-transcending to be truly courageous about.

—Ernest Becker (*Beyond alienation*, 1967, p. 213)

Imagine a world where carnival and the fluid center permeate, a world where Toby could come fully into his own, which means that he could maximally enter "into" himself and the regions formerly blocked off from himself. What would such a world look like? How would the sectors of power be constituted, individual and social lives be arrayed?

Idle fantasies you muse? Pie in the sky, totally cut off from reality you object? Perhaps, but, on the other hand, we do not fantasize enough about such potentialities, and perhaps it is time to *translate* more of that which is merely theorized in the social sciences. This was certainly the concern of Becker.[14] Without an ideal-typical model, he asserted, there could be no advancement in social research.

There are, moreover, some existing models that we can draw on. The Council for a Parliament of the World Religions, an ecumenical organization of religious and scientific constituents, has recently proposed a compelling declaration of principles. This declaration is intended for display at public institutions worldwide to remind people of its urgent and abiding message. Known formally as a "global ethic," the declaration calls for the world's "guiding institutions"—government, business, academia, and so on—to support the following interfaith resolution:

"Together, we affirm [the sense of awe—humility, reverence, and wonder—toward all being and] the [following] four fundamental commitments...*

1. Commitment to a Culture of Non-Violence and Respect for Life.
2. Commitment to a Culture of Solidarity and Just Economic Order.
3. Commitment to a Culture of Tolerance and Life of Truthfulness.
4. Commitment to a Culture of Equal Rights and Partnership between Men and Women." (Council for a Parliament of the World Religions, 1999)[15]

When I speak of conditions for a fluid center, then, to what specifically do I refer? I refer to the context within which our smallness and greatness can be recognized in their vividness, their fullness.

---

* The clause within the brackets is my own addendum, suggested at a meeting of local members of the Parliament 11/9/99 in Berkeley, CA.

This is a view that acknowledges smallness without squelching the potential for greatness (fluidity, expansion) and that affirms greatness without denying the equally relevant necessity for smallness (containment, centeredness). It is a view exemplified by the most accomplished philosophers, scientists, and artisans, who are at the same time the most reverent agnostics, seekers, and inquirers. Likewise, it is illustrated by the most oppressed and challenged victims, who, with time and great effort, can transform into the most resilient visionaries. Put summarily: The context of awe, of appreciation, and of discernment promotes the richest possible range of experience within the most suitable parameters of support; it maximizes elasticity, while minimizing polarity and regret.

Despite the vigor of this scenario, readers are probably asking what so many of us wonder when we entertain such flights of fancy—how can the ideals be *implemented*? Below I reply generally, then specifically, to this query.

As previously suggested, the first principle we must attend to is that of our paradoxical condition. We must acknowledge both our smallness and our greatness—our concerns about mattering (but not too much!)—in the practical application of our thesis.

With respect to acknowledging our smallness (our needs for safety, support, and structure), I join the chorus of calls for an increased safety net in our society. Just as in carnival, there need to be provisions for health, housing, a dignified form of charity (such as workfare for those who are capable), and a greatly improved minimum wage. I think we also need to institute curbs on entrepreneurial and corporate domination. If we have the faintest hope that those at the bottom and middle will sacrifice, we need to stress the moral and spiritual *obligation* of those at the top to those who helped them get there, the spirit of "return." The way to do this is probably through incentives, not penalties. In other words, give such ambitious types massive tax breaks for minority hiring or for giving to socially beneficial programs. And make the alternatives to embracing such incentives (and values) sting—such as would be accomplished by onerous taxation. (How many millions do people really need?) The issue here is to shift the emphasis from a sense of acquisitiveness to a sense of participation and from a sense of reward through materialism to reward through social-spiritual service.

To address our need for greatness—for discovery, adventure, and innovation—and for *embodied meaning*, I propose a list of priorities. This list would be arrived at by consensus (through local referenda perhaps) and would comprise a wide range of social tasks. Beyond simply rebuilding the infrastructure of the country—housing, roads, mass transit, clean-up of the environment—there would be a genuine stress on *creative* engagement of those and other tasks. There could be provisions, for example, for citywide mentorship programs for the underprivileged, such as has been demonstrated in some communities by male African American mentors for young boys. In addition to stressing community service, this mentorship could also accent relationship building, job diversification, and aesthetic city planning. To increase students' attention spans, there could be prominent reductions in class sizes, especially in inner city ghettos. Such reductions have been called urgent by many of those who teach and administer in such settings. There could be an infusion of performing arts and humanities programs for public school children generally. Such programs would attempt to bring alive the treasure-house of wisdom from literature and could be great fun to communally produce. There could be community-service programs of all kinds, especially for college-age youths, and perhaps tied to their education to facilitate these and other programs.

Two recent studies, in fact, uphold the value of these kinds of performing arts and mentorship programs. Both of these studies are contained in a June 2003 report issued by the Institute for Urban and Minority Education of Teacher's College, Columbia University. The Institute's report, entitled, "Changing the Script for Youth Development, An Evaluation of the All Stars Talent Show Network and the Joseph A. Forgione Development School for Youth" (by E. Gordon, C. Bonilla Bowman, & B. Mejia), shows emphatically that fun, "developmentally driven" performing arts and apprenticeship programs can have salutary effects on some of the poorest urban youth (p. 110). In particular, the above two programs yielded "powerfully constructive" results in the areas of community building, self-confidence, and self-presentation (p. 111).

With respect to the vocational setting, there could be much more meaningful worker participation. Such participation could include actual joint ownership, input on lay-offs or pay-cuts, and input on overall operations. There could and need to be shorter work weeks and thereby expanded opportunities for employees to spend time with families or outside interests.

Finally, there could be an infusion of opportunities for employees to substantively reflect on their lives. Such reflection could take the form of meditation retreats, encounter groups, or depth-experiential therapies (e.g., therapies that stress embodied self-awareness). The idea of these offerings would be to reconnect employees with the purpose and meaning of their lives and, as a result, the social-vocational contexts within which they dwell. Among the many presumed benefits of such a reconnection would be improvements in intra- and interpersonal communication, relationships, and health. There would also likely be improvements in employee motivation, cohesion, and resonance with jobs. Society as a whole would likely reap the rewards of such enhancement in the forms of reduced criminality, increased respectfulness toward self, others, and the environment, and enhanced creativity.

How then do we impel the powers that be to move in these ambitious directions? We need to be pragmatically frank: We need to make plain that due to the rising tide of disenfranchisement, disillusionment, and alienation in our society—and the world— *failure* to create carnival means revolution, pure and simple.

Is this failure not related to the recent terrorist attacks on U.S. embassies and, more recently, the World Trade Center and Pentagon? While there clearly can be no justification for these egregious acts, they must be seen, at least tacitly, as the backlashes of the dispossessed, as twisted and maniacal rage reactions against industrialist, materialist, and hegemonic Western values.[16] Among these values are the hoarding of Middle Eastern oil reserves (at the expense of war and atrocity),[17] Western exploitation of indigenous workforces, the propagation of corrupt or elitist alliances, and the exploitation of the environment for capital gain. Similarly the recent accounting fiascos at Enron and Worldcom do not advance the Western cause.

We can do better, and we can provide models that aspire to better: arousing less hate and more curiosity, less estrangement and more interchange. Heinous and warped as backlashes to our system may be, they must be seen in their fullness, as distress signals, alerting us not just to root out the enemy, but to face the enemy within.

The more immediate tack we could take—at least here in America—is to persuade the powers that be that the taxes we levy and the range of projects for which they are designated will be scrupulously monitored. We should ensure that whatever taxes are earmarked for, they will be used for, *period*. Not only government, but also all interested parties, including taxpayers and the groups they fund, should be integral to this monitoring process.

At the risk of sounding overly Pollyannaish about this ideal-typical world, let us elaborate on its grittier realities—and those leading up to it. The first such reality is that people are fed up with the class and income disparities in the world, particularly in America. This is a condition where in 1999 nineteen percent of American children lived in poverty (the worst rate in the developed world); where in 1997 the average American CEO made 326 times what the average factory worker made; and where in 1992 the top 2.7 percent of wage earners made as much as the bottom 100 million.[18] It's a world where a camp counselor can and often does earn more than a frontline mental health worker at a home for disturbed children (personal communication, Sebastian Earl, 1999), or an information technologist makes several times the salary of a social worker, or a professional basketball player makes ten times the wages of a teacher. These income disparities are not just glaring; they're appalling. They are direct reflections of an awe-depleted, thoroughly myopic culture. If we spent a fraction of the wealth we invest in maintaining extravagant, materially saturated lifestyles, in social, emotional, and physical development programs, not only would we elevate the well-being of millions, but we would also bolster the prospects for their children and generations to come. Further, we would markedly decrease criminality, disease, and environmental abuse, while at the same time expanding personal and interpersonal satisfaction, zeal, motivation, and production.[19]

This condition has a particular poignancy right now, as we ponder our response to the terrorist attacks on New York City and the Pentagon. These were heinous and unspeakable crimes, and the perpetrators of these crimes should be dealt with accordingly. But in our haste to seek retribution, we should not neglect to reassess our own bull-headed policies, which in many ways may have contributed to our current lot.

America is a genuinely great experiment; it possesses the underpinnings of a world-transforming community—a community where the interests of the individual are balanced against those of the collective, and vice versa, and where freedom, diversity, and socio-cultural interchange can genuinely flourish. However, the barriers to this ideal relate directly to our economic structure. While capitalism in itself may not be the culprit, it is *our form* of capitalism that constricts, distorts, and subverts our foundational aims. You can't incessantly treat human beings as capital, as instruments of financial, material, or political gain, and expect to court their sympathy; there will be fallout from these actions, and it will not be palatable.

To be sure, there is no ready solution to this situation; it is endemic and pervasive. Yet change could occur in the long run, if we are able to counterbalance materialist strivings with those that respect people. A number of social experiments have shown that, even in the most adversarial circumstances, when people can assemble together, share experiences, and learn about each other's intimate lives, they become more tolerant of one another and more appreciative of one another's humanity.[20]

If we are to have a chance at global solidarity, then we need a palpable change in our relations to capital. We need to complement such relations with a new set of conditions. Among these conditions would be the routine availability of interpersonal exchange—the sharing of joys and sorrows, hopes and estrange-ments—within a supportive, society-wide infrastructure. Then, and only then, in my view could the primeval engines of capital-ism—drive and self-initiative—be honed and socially redeemed.

Our culture is remiss not to recognize these glaring implica-tions, not only because they are substantive and empirically based, but also because they are practical and economically vital. Consider what is at stake here: the short-term and cosmetic boost of the few versus the long-term and robust uplift of the many. There is little doubt that our current path is a recipe for annihilation, both of self and other. The more we hoard, the more we adorn, the more we privilege, and the more we neglect, the readier we court hate, divi-sion, and anarchy. The result will be that no matter how many ty-coons we create, no matter how many glittering machines we build, and no matter how many armies we amass, they will all amount to dust before the backlashes of the dispossessed.

We profess to desire an engaged and invigorated citizenry. We say we want an informed and unified populace. We advertise our yen for physically and emotionally healthy children, youth who are committed to the values of work and brotherly love. Yet despite our rhetoric, we have a very puzzling way of demonstrating our concerns. How is it, for example, as suggested earlier, that our eco-nomic system is virtually tailor-made to subvert our alleged values, and how is it that our morals, relationships, and lifestyles are for all intents and purposes contrary to our pronouncements?

To be sure, I am hardly the first to point out the grave hypoc-risies in our system of governance. There have been many before me who have valiantly cried out for reform only to meet with de-rision, cynicism, or worse. One difference in this appeal, however, is that although it is radical, it does not, at least in the short run, call for radical restructuring.

With a few strategically placed exceptions—the implications of which are frankly colossal—notable changes can be made within the existing market framework. Again, there are a number of possi-ble alternatives, including tax incentives, to achieve this end. These are alternatives designed to alert and sensitize but not disable the extraordinarily rich. They are intended to limit but not eradicate the motivation for material gain. At the same time, however, they are intended to turn the sights of those who have "made it" to those upon whom their "success" was built (e.g., the citizenry at large) and, in a more general sense, to the whole question of "success." The challenge that is posed is whether conventional notions of success can be converted into visionary conceptions—whether "wealth" can mean capacity for humility, reverence, and wonder—awe—before creation?

4

Toward an Awe-Based Work Policy

Life and livelihood ought not to be separated but to flow from the same source, which is Spirit, for life and livelihood are about Spirit.

—Matthew Fox (*Reinvention of work: A new vision of livelihood for our times*, New York: HarperCollins, 1994, p. 1)

What follows is a vision. It is not a hard and fast blueprint for the reformation of work, but a stimulus for discussion. It is one proposal for change that may inspire other, more concrete proposals, to revive our moribund system.

The first step toward an awe-based transformation of work, then, might entail the following: the provision of an awe-based, socially responsible well-being program for both workers and their employers. The intent of this initiative, for those who support it, would be to re-instill a sense of awe—a sense of the reverence and passion for work—through both dialogue and activity.

The well-being programs would comprise both a mental and physical component, and they would be administered by a committee. This committee could include the employer, mental and physical health providers (e.g., psychologists, psychiatrists, counselors, general practice physicians, holistic health practitioners), and employees. The programs would be voluntary and scheduled once a week for one hour respectively. The mental well-being program could entail a wide variety of offerings, from topics of psychological and philosophical interest to those concerning spirituality and multiculturalism. The purpose of the mental well-being programs would be to promote reflection on and, where appropriate, take corrective action concerning the impact of work on employees' and employers' lives. Although such reflection and corrective action would be confined to work issues, they could address a range of concerns. For example, the program might take the form of a discussion hour in which employers and employees consider the environmental relevance of their products. It could also take the form of a reflection about the need to restore pride, craftsmanship, and innovation at the work site. Also it could entail motivational seminars or forums about social values. The mental well-being programs would need to fulfill four basic criteria. They would need to be 1) independently facilitated (e.g., by a licensed mental health professional); 2) voluntary and non-discriminatory (e.g., protected from employer retaliation); 3) relevant to the work setting; and 4) acceptable to an employee appointed well-being committee. (For issues that fall outside these categories, other healthcare/organizational services may be necessitated.) Finally, the well-being committee would, through one of its elected representatives, have a permanent seat on the respective company's board.

The physical well-being programs would also consist of a variety of offerings and would be administered by a physical well-being committee. The committee would consist of the employer, an elected body of employees, and a physical health expert of their choice. Activities could range from workout regimens to massage and sauna to yoga and stress-reduction exercises. There could also be provisions for a variety of programs on holistic health, exercise, nutrition, and alternative medicines. The on-staff health provider would help to monitor and, if necessary, medically advise all participants.

In addition to the above programs, there could be provisions for a range of alternative activities during the mental and physical well-being hours, from nature walks to outdoor retreats to communal projects (such as consumer satisfaction surveys). Those who decide not to partake in such activities would also have a variety of options from which to choose, from relaxing and recreating to continuing work.

In order to maximize the integration of work and personal activity, four and one half day work weeks could be implemented.

Such a period could provide vital time for reflection, for loved ones, and for recreation. It also structures time for those who wish to partake in civic or communal involvement (which is highly truncated today, and a major point of social critique). Further, such hours allow additional time for those who wish to cultivate outside interests such as hobbies, crafts, or arts.

Possible Scenarios

Envision, if you will, a work setting where there are weekly "discussion hours" to air philosophical concerns, where health and exercise are encouraged, and where workers have a consistent say in operations. Imagine a setting where ethical philosophers hold monthly seminars and depth-psychologists work intimately with employees to reflect on their lives. This is a work-site that prizes meaningfulness as much or more than making a profit and as a byproduct of its emphasis generally becomes profitable in spite of itself. Envision an entire nation, perhaps even world, of such invigorated vocational settings; consider the lives that would be touched, the educative and communal possibilities offered, and the diversity of perspectives interwoven. The following is one vision of an awe-based/well-being-focused work setting.

Picture our earlier subject, Toby, at 25 years of age. He has healed from many of his wounds and he has evolved into a fit and enterprising young man. Toby is a copy editor at a publishing firm. He reads manuscripts to determine their compatibility with his company's philosophy and he proofreads texts that have been cleared for publication. Toby has a full and intriguing schedule. In addition to his reading duties, he also participates in a weekly mental well-being program (which includes a discussion hour), as well as a weekly physical well-being regimen (which includes yoga). Moreover, on the occasion when he feels down or emotionally conflicted, he visits a staff therapist or consults with an ethical philosopher.

Today Toby is attending a discussion hour. "We have a profound ethical dilemma," Toby's colleague, Mortimer, declares to the group. "While our company devotes great quantities of energy to producing quality books, books that inform, challenge, and illuminate, there has been a curious drop in sales to the teen market. Now what the hell is going on? Just two years ago our works were going gang buster with these kids, but in the last eighteen months they have been buying comic books and computer manuals!" At that moment, there is a hush over the group. The group leader, a psychologist, looks on with curiosity. Suddenly, an older colleague interjects, "Thanks for your concern, Mortimer, and for letting us know the situation. But why don't you take a moment to catch your breath and take a look at this thing in a larger light. My feeling is that there is a reason these kids aren't buying our 'substantive' works and that we ought to take a look at that reason before jumping to too many conclusions." Another co-worker pipes up, "Yeah, and it may well be that this whole situation is temporary and that the kids will become saturated by that other stuff. Why don't we do depth interviews and find out more about what they want. In the meantime, our other productions should keep us afloat."

The above vignette illustrates the thoughtfulness, openness, and security that are likely to be exhibited within fluidly centered organizations. Mortimer has some legitimate fears about the viability of the publishing program, but the atmosphere of dialogue and reflection enables others to place his concerns in context. As the older co-workers suggested, there doesn't have to be an atmosphere of panic about the teen market. The publishing company does not have to pander to sudden market shifts. Because there is a safety net in this hypothesized society, and because the company itself has cultivated meaningful and enduring products, it has the luxury of both time and forethought. Further, the company's luxury of time allows it to study the marketing issue in depth. Instead of ordering some cheap, quick, quantitative surveys of consumer needs, for example, it can mobilize a richly descriptive, subtly nuanced qualitative exploration of such needs. Such a study would tease out the context for otherwise simplistic or stereotypic findings. It is conventionally assumed in our own

statistics-obsessed culture, for example, that teens prefer literature that is laden with sex, fighting, and recklessness. Yet, an in-
depth qualitative investigation of teen preferences might reveal a
very different understanding. For example, Toby's company may
find in their qualitative inquiry that what teens genuinely desire
is literature that "speaks" to their sexual, physical, and adventurous identities, and that the current line of books falls short of
these needs. Hence, it may be that the stick-figure depictions of
sex, drug-taking, and rock and roll that turn up in conventional
surveys do not at all reflect the essence of teens' preferences. That
which may resonate, on the other hand, could be contemporary
and culturally attuned dramas, parables that raise intelligent
questions about teens' hopes and fears, their imaginations, and
their budding sexuality. Based on this in-depth, qualitative information, then, Toby's company can reassess its perceptions about
the teen market, and, as a result, ethically and intelligently address
a new and potentially more relevant teen readership.

To be sure, this speculation may well fall short of the mark.
It may be, by contrast, that cheap and visceral thrills are precisely what teens crave and that a market that caters to such tastes is
necessitated. In a fluidly centered society, however, I doubt that
there would be a need of such fare. This is because, in the spirit
of carnival, there would be thrills aplenty in such a world, simply through the natural course of living. Moreover, there would
be an openness to the dark, the uncanny, and the wondrous,
both at home and at work. Communication and expression
would be prized in such a society, and so would experimentation. If, from young ages children are assisted to acknowledge
the primal—wind, stars, rain, death, loss, anxiety, desire, guilt,
suffering—there will be less need to control, indulge in, or appropriate the primal in later life. The recognition of the significance of time will have a great deal to do with this enlarged
consciousness. To the degree that parents are encouraged to
incorporate pauses, curiosities, and adventures into their lives,
children will benefit immensely.

Seven blocks from Toby's company, there is another discussion hour taking place. At Blakey's, a local fast food restaurant, workers are questioning the nutritional value of their service. Company employers are listening closely, for they are acutely aware that such discussion hours have been taking place all over the city and they have become integral to corporate personnel policies. Increasingly, moreover, they are finding that employees' demands for nutritious food are being met by receptive ears, and concrete changes are being implemented throughout the food industry. Although Blakey's is one of the slower outfits to swing around to the growing calls, it is a study par excellence of the discussion hour's impact and hands-on influence on company higher-ups.

The psychologist running this particular discussion hour at Blakey's begins with evocative questions: "What really matters to you today about your work; how is what you do important?" With that said, two of the twenty employees gathered on this autumn afternoon raise their hand. Ellen speaks first: "As much as my supervisors may not want to hear this, I am at wits' end with the lies we're telling in our ads, the food we're serving at our stores, and the sicknesses we're witnessing in our communities as a result. Fast food places all over the area are recognizing the great value of nutritious, health-giving additions to their menus, and some, in fact, are even changing their regular menus. Yet we continue to roll out these synthesized, lard-ridden cholesterol boosters to any one, any time, who's willing to pay. Last week I buried my 55-year-old uncle who, as many of you know, gorged himself on these junk foods for the last 25 years. Now I'm not saying that his blocked valves were a direct result of his daily lunches at Blakey's, but I'll be damned if there isn't a strong connection! Everyday we're getting reports about the sluggishness and obesity of the American lifestyle; everyday people are clogging hospitals with circulatory problems and binging themselves sick on French fries, burgers, and cola—and here we're glorifying them. Don't we get the message?"

The other worker with his hand up, John, pipes in: "Yeah, Ellen, I know exactly where you're coming from. I just went to my doctor the other day and he put me on hypertension pills and told me to lay off the junk food. I've been having more and more questions about what we are really doing here at this corporation. We sell our kids grease, throw a clown in our ads, and a playground in our stores, and they think we're angels. But we may be killing some of these people—we're committing a slow homicide. It's definitely time for a change."

The psychologist looks over the group and halts for a moment. Then he begins, "Let's all take a moment to reflect on the experiences of Ellen and John. Are there any other feelings about Blakey's menu? This is your chance to take stock." Another worker speaks up: "You know, I haven't really given it the thought it deserves, but one of the things I've always liked about this place is the kids. The kids descend on this place at the lunch hour and they're always so full of energy and idealism. I hear the Markus boys jawing about the basketball team they're joining, and a guy named Max reflecting on his favorite science class. I hear all kinds of stories and all kinds of lives. I hate to be thinking that we're really hurting these kids, or adults, who simply come to us to enjoy a meal in a fun and cozy atmosphere." There are many nodding heads following this statement.

The manager of the restaurant interjects, "OK, I think I've heard enough to realize that we've been heading down an ill-fated track. How about this, I'll present your concerns at the next supervisors meeting and also convey them to the president of the corporation. Second, let's invite a nutritionist (whom a subcommittee of us can agree upon) to come and speak to us at our next discussion hour. Perhaps this person can offer some concrete tips about how to redesign our service. At least this is where we can begin."

Practical Aspects

Are the well-being programs delusional, socially and economically crippling? I think not. While it is true that about two hours would be subtracted from the conventional work-week, the two hours that would replace them should be more than enough to make up for such a loss; in fact, they should form the bedrock for a revolutionary new form of living. In these two hours people would be encouraged to reflect deeply on—and reinvigorate—their jobs, their lives, and the lives of those about them. The fruits of such engagement should be manifold, from enhancement of the work environment to humanization of the social terrain, and from improved vocational motivation to elevated social and moral sensitivity. The services resulting from such a transformation should also be markedly improved. There should be more services, for example, that address people's core values, such as environmentally supportive transportation programs, life-enhancing architectural arrangements, and health-affirming agricultural yields. There should be marked improvements in mental and physical health, race relations, and education. There should be more and better medical services, with a wider range of treatment alternatives (for example, low cost, year-long psychotherapy).

There should be pervasive improvements in recreational facilities, entertainment, and sporting events. There should be dramatically fewer overpaid executives, entertainers, and athletes and markedly increased affordability of products and services. For example, to the extent that products become more meaningful to people, they will buy them more, which in turn should lower prices; and to the degree that entrepreneurial wealth is returned to the system that supports it, the quality and affordability of that system should also commensurately rise.

The well-being programs also open up unprecedented opportunities for specialists in human service, from psychologists to physicians, philosophers to artisans, and counselors to healers. While some may decry the ferocity of that transformation, I would argue that it is just the counterweight necessitated today, as technical models for living encroach upon the cultural landscape. With this slight modification, then, the entire tenor of Western, but particularly American culture could transform; the entire Calvinist, rationalist, and patriarchal hierarchy could topple. And in their stead, a whole new socio-political prioritization could emerge, a prioritization that prizes people over profits, human beings over devices, lives over statistics, relationships over "business," and amazement over efficiency. To be sure, awe-based prioritization should not eliminate the former technicist model. It should not erase the significant and hard-won gains of industrialization such as controlling diseases, mass producing food, and expediting information. Such a call would be sheer folly, and few, if any of the people urging humanistic change would seriously entertain it. However, an awe-based reform should bring a deepening, a sensitizing, and a widening of our day-to-day view. It should instill the fluidity in the inert centeredness and the flesh, bone, and heart in the pale plurality of our culture.

Who, in our material-minded society, would actually endorse, let alone accept, the well-being vision? In actuality, I believe that many people would, particularly if the idea is well-articulated. Foremost among the people who should welcome the well-being vision would be employees, but the support would not end there. Although many employers would balk at the expenditure of such a program, others would soon realize that employee motivation, attendance, and production, would all be enhanced within the awe-based context, and so would the production line itself. Moreover, both employer and employee would soon find that there would still be room for healthy profit and wage earnings in spite of, and perhaps even in light of, the increased social consciousness at a given work-setting (e.g., because of the greater social relevance of that setting's structure and product line). Last, but not least, most, if not all, prospective workers will have undergone an awe-based educational regimen (discussed momentarily). They would, therefore, be inclined to value rather than to discount a vocational analogue of the latter.

Social Gains

With a new priority on humanity, then, how else would the culture function, and who else would lead us in this transformation? This is a vast query, of course, but the outlines of a response are visible.

At the start of Herb Gardener's (1965) animated (and pitifully neglected) screenplay *A Thousand Clowns,* an unemployed comedy writer, Murray, leads his 11-year-old nephew, Nick, to an empty Manhattan street. It is the hour of daybreak, and as they stare into the cavernous depths, Murray suddenly turns to Nick and bellows: "In a moment you're going to see a horrible thing." "What's that?," the boy asks. "People are going to work!", Murray replies. While the levity in Murray's voice is obvious, the gravity of the point may not be. Murray is America's Zorba and the voice he reflects is pure Nietzschean.

The problem with "business as usual" is that The Great Conversation—the dialogues of Plato, the poetry of Dante, the musings of Milton, Shakespeare, Goethe, and Schiller, and, more recently, William James, John Dewey, Richard Rorty, Mohandas Gandhi, W.E.B. DuBois, Martin Luther King, Jr., James Baldwin, Maya Angelou, Isabel Allende, and countless others who fill our globe with inspiration—gets almost completely lost. It gets lost because it is sparingly disseminated today and sparingly required. Like the Latin and Greek languages, The Great Conversation of philosophy and religion, of art and literature, and of life itself lacks all the voguish elements—speed, packaging, and instant results.

Yet, as we have seen with the recent attacks on the World Trade Towers and Pentagon, there may be a daimonic backlash against these trends. When Rollo May writes that "dialogue" is one of the most vital hedges against the daimonic return of the repressed in our culture, The Great Conversation is a part of that to which he refers.[1] The daimonic, according to May, is any natural function or life-force that has the capacity to take over our whole being. Practically any emotion—anger, fear, sadness—can fulfill this definition, as can any intensified concern. While the daimonic can be life-giving, it can also be life-destroying, and it must be dealt with accordingly. The trigger for life-destroying daimonism is dichotomization, the cutting off of experience. To the extent that we repress experience, then the more it is susceptible to turbulent backlashes. To the extent that we encounter, embrace, and grapple with experience, on the other hand, then the more stable it tends to be. To put the problem in the current parlance, the more that we repress our needs for inspiration, for The Great Conversation, and for awareness about who and what we are, what we dream of, and what we deeply desire, the more we court division, fragmentation, and ultimately collapse.

From this point of view, it is essential that we maintain The Great Conversation, and not just in the ivory tower but in the streets and suites as well. The well-being proposal releases unprecedented creative energies for individual and social expression—within the existing structures of a disciplined and committed workforce. The range of possibilities arising from the well-being forums will be rich, for not only will various companies opt for diverse presentations, but also various Great Conversations within those presentations will impact company policymaking. Put another way, The Great Conversation should lead to a continually evolving network of ideas, expressions, and sensibilities, which lead, in turn, to an ever-growing sphere of personal and vocational participation. Where will all this lead?

The convergence of an awe-based, meaning-based, and reflection-based pause in the middle of people's workday should only be the beginning. Not only private business but government and educational systems, nonprofits, and volunteer agencies should all be encouraged to follow suit. At the same time, however, we must not be dictatorial about this transformation. This should not become another one of those disastrous social engineering projects. We do not want the well-being programs to become Walden II, or forced collectivization, or the New Soviet Man. To the contrary, we have learned aplenty from these robotic exercises, and the lesson is that change must evolve from within; it can neither be dictated nor imposed.[2]

The idea, then, is to create conditions for radical social transformation, a seedbed for fluidly centered, awe-inspired living. The task is to craft a program that will mobilize people, that will spark their imagination, and that will move them to act. Reflection on the meaning of peoples' vocations for their own and others' lives is truly a start on the road to substantive individual and social change. Consider further the likely chain of developments that would ensue from such a catalyst. To the extent that they give input and utilize their representation with management, individuals will feel that they have a stake in company operations. Second, men and women will face each other as people, rather than as mechanized stereotypes. Managers will discover the concerns and values of employees; employees will discover the desires and hesitancies of managers; Caucasians will discover the humanity of people of color, and vice versa, and all will unveil the dreams, visions, and ethical leanings of each other. In time, there may even be a diminishment of the necessity for union representation, as such representation (and beyond) will be integral to day-to-day business.

The animation and invigoration of work-life is bound to pay off large dividends on the social and domestic fronts. To the degree that workers feel vocationally empowered, challenged, and enlightened, they are also more likely to feel interested and engaged at home, in their neighborhoods, and in their cultures. Gone will be the festering hostility toward one's job or co-worker, the frustration with the emptiness of one's days, and the oppressive estrangement from one's environment. In turn, there will be less bitterness about the demands of home-life, less cynicism about the integrity of neighbors or public officials, and decreased resentment about time or personal freedom.

5

A Return to Basics: Awe-Based Education

But one thing we here must agree upon, and that is the need for education to hold up to [humanity] the vision of the *absolutely* serious; the awesome, the mighty, the all-transcending, the divine mystery in all its unspeakable magnitude—this, and only this, is fit to call upon the energies of free [people]. This, and only this, gives life its dignity and its tragedy, its joy and its weight, its sense of abysmal limitation, and somehow limitless opportunity. The all-transcending mystery of the cosmic process is the only possible direction of the thrust of life, and hence of the possibility of freedom—whatever it may ultimately mean. Again, we are reminded of Augustine's idea that unless [people] looked in this direction, [they were] hopelessly *curvatas*, somehow less than fully human, fetishized and bent upon narrow and ignoble things. This was the difference between *cupiditas* and *caritas*, of love for things and love for God. And what is "love" for any living creature, except the sentiment that the universe is alive and significant,—alive and significant according to the creature's own living energies.

—Ernest Becker (*Beyond alienation*, 1967, pp. 211–212)

The real beginning of education must be the experimental realization of absolute mystery.

—R. Buckminster Fuller (*Intuition*, San Luis Obispo, CA:
Impact, 1983, p. 61)

For all their dynamism, the vocational well-being programs are delimited. They must be complemented by an educational or developmental component that informs and precedes them. Again,

however, here, as ever, we must proceed cautiously. We must not
be heavy-handed about this and fall into the error of "pushing"
an ill-fitting curriculum—such as that of the "mental hygiene"
movement in the early 1920s, or the "Great Books" movement of
the 1930s, or the "open classroom" and "back to basics" trends of
the 1970s and 1980s. The pivotal issue here is how to maintain,
enhance, and refine that which Rudolf Otto has so well termed
our "innermost core"—our capacity for awe.[1] Howard Thurman,
a noted San Francisco theologian put it this way:

> "Ask not what the world needs, rather ask what makes you
> come alive and go do that, for what the world needs is people
> who have come alive."[2]

In his phenomenal revision of public education, *Beyond
alienation,* Ernest Becker suggests that to be truly democratic,
curricula would have to meet three criteria—they would have to
be liberating, philosophically critical, and presently relevant.[3] By
liberating, Becker means that courses would have to mean something, to matter to students. They would have to open new doors
of possibility to students, give them new ways of thinking about
old problems. Put succinctly, such curricula would need to emphasize discovery, not mechanics and regurgitation. For Becker,
the biggest problem with traditional education, and with culture
in general, is that it "fetishizes." Fetishization is the narrowing
down and confinement of thoughts, feelings, and sensations. It
is the confinement of subject matter to that which is peripheral
or institutional. It is the cosmetic or anxiety-riddled "solution"
versus the complex and rich reflection; it promotes elitism,
scapegoating, and atrophy. The embrace of big and meaningful
questions on the other hand—questions such as who we are, what
deeply matters to us, and where we are headed—are the contexts
for a liberating curriculum.

By philosophically critical, Becker refers to the need for rigorous analysis of history and culture: What has worked and what has
failed, what has lifted us from oppression, and what has crushed

us? What has brought us fulfillment, and what has dampened our spirits? What has beckoned us forward, and what has laid us low? A philosophically critical curriculum, then, would weigh the respective impact of every major epoch of history, every major Eastern and Western worldview, and every notable global crisis.

The confluence of emancipatory and critical education, however, are not enough for Becker. To be truly democratic, truly freeing, education must also be relevant. The question is to what extent courses pertain to our current situation in the world, and more importantly, to each and every student who engages them? Put another way, to what extent does the curriculum provide a lens through which each student can learn about her or his own life, her or his own failings, anxieties, triumphs?

This formulation is what Becker provocatively terms his "alienation curriculum." The alienation curriculum is a foundational study of the diverse forms of human estrangement, the means by which to overcome that condition, and the relevance of those means to contemporary humanity.

Drawing from Becker's proposal, I will now set forth a proposal of my own, a proposal to enhance and complement the movement toward a fluid center at work, at home, and in places of worship. This proposal is for an awe-based[4] educational curriculum. Like Becker's, this curriculum would explore the historical, social, and personal dimensions of human liberation, but unlike Becker's scenario, which is somewhat general in character, this awe-based program would outline specifics. While Becker speaks eloquently of the estrangement from and engagement with human freedom, he really does not give us a guideline or mooring post by which to evaluate such an attainment. I propose that the capacity for awe—for humility, reverence, and wonder—gives us such a guideline. To the extent that a curriculum promotes awe—the cultivation of students' deepest sensibilities, the capacity to grapple with those sensibilities, and the capacity to develop a stance in the context of that discovery and grappling—it is a maximally liberating curriculum. Such a curriculum, in other words, would enable students to encounter their deepest fears, fantasies, and curiosities about who they are, where they came from, and whither they are headed. It would enable them to explore and discern the kinds of lifestyles, worldviews, and historical epochs that make sense for their individual and collective lives and that would lead, presumably, to a dynamic calling.

What is freedom but accessibility for these students? It is accessibility on all the major levels—from the physiological to the cognitive and from the interpersonal to the psychospiritual. And what is accessibility ultimately but the back and forth tussle between doubt and faith, mystery and passion, and the resultant strengths, resiliencies, and purposes that ensue?

There will, of course, be individual variation in response to such an evocative curriculum, but there will also be many checks and balances built into it. For example, it would be difficult in such an atmosphere for students to become intractably extreme or parochial. On the contrary, the contradictory, the puzzling, and the discomfiting will be inherent to their inquiry, as will the uplifting and inspiriting.

Such an education would breathe new life into the philosophy memorialized by Paul Tillich—and every other great existential philosopher—which was to bring "doubt to the faithful and faith to the doubters."[5] More importantly, such an education revives the notion of theonomy, an idea significant for Tillich and Becker and alluded to by Nietzsche and Heidegger.[6] It revives precisely humanity's boldness, dignity, and possibility in all its befuddling fragility.

Given the above, then, two questions naturally arise: Who would be the architect of this awe-based course design? and What students could realistically engage it? Following the lead of Becker's student-run curriculum and Ortega's Faculty of Culture,[7] I would propose that each school district develop its own "awe advocacy agency." Ideally, such an agency (or committee) would be composed of a multi-ethnic amalgam of faculty, students, and select members of the community. The task of this agency would be to advise teachers about how best to present a timely, significant, and relevant awe-based curriculum to the local student population. The guiding questions with which both the agency and teachers would need to grapple would be: First, what are the key historical epochs, and how did the peoples (or cultures) in those epochs stifle or promote the cultivation of awe? Second, what are the aspects of those dynamics that are relevant to contemporary student lives?

Now there is a catch here. Not just any curriculum under the rubric of awe advocacy can be proposed or adopted. Neither dogmatism nor sectarianism would be sanctioned in such an ethos, and the democratic principle of separating church from state would be sacrosanct. The reason for this injunction is simple, and it follows from that which has been previously discussed: Awe requires maximal access to experience—it necessitates thoroughly open inquiry—and such access and inquiry can only thrive in a democracy. To ensure the establishment of the aforementioned, an overseer, such as a national awe advocacy agency could be created. This agency—also composed of academics, students, and concerned citizens, each elected by their peers and underwritten by the government—would set the standards for all the local awe advocacy agencies, as well as the curricula they recommend. An example of these standards might be a core curriculum that all public schools would be required to teach. Such a curriculum would spell out the mission of an awe-based curriculum, the democratic (as opposed to moralizing) manner in which courses are to be taught, and the essential content to be covered, e.g., reading, writing, math and science, literature and the arts, and history.

As for which students would be prepared for such a philosophically challenging curriculum, I have several thoughts. First, because the capacity for awe is native to us, and because it is as much if not more a component of early childhood as it is of later youth, such a curriculum should be integral from the start. Indeed, it should take center stage from children's entrance into preschool and expand out from there. To be sure, there would still be a necessity for "nuts and bolts" and even rote learning. Just as now, students would need to acquire the basic skills of reading, writing, and arithmetic. However, the whole thrust of the academic project, the whole thinking about education, would need to transform. It would need to move from an emphasis on technical competence to an accent on values, personal meaning, and inquiry. It would need to shift from a stress on remote and distant learning to personal, hands-on discovery. (For an example of this style of learning, see the December 2, 1991 article in *Newsweek* magazine, pp. 53–54, on the Reggio Emilia approach to early education.) While the technical and specialty training would be incorporated into primary education, it would not be fully emphasized until the latter stages of the student's career. Here and only here could it be richly informed by her awe-inspired knowledge base. Here and only here could the student draw on a wealth of details about what crushes and aggrandizes, and what enlivens and energizes, the human spirit. A student interested in becoming a medical doctor, for example, would draw on a bountiful range of awareness. She will have reflected profoundly about history and culture, healing and suffering, and will bring these to bear on her studies. This knowledge however will not just be about others, but also about her own hard-won realizations and her own time-leavened discoveries. It will be rigorously informed by books and dialogues, but also by field trips, forays into museums, and hands-on drawings, sculptings, and dramatizations. The student's medical specialty, therefore, is not likely to be a mere skill or tool for external ends, but an integral part of her interest in the world and that which calls her to the world. The result would be an awe-informed capacity to identify and minister to ill people, not merely to illness. Later, we will elaborate the details of such a vocation.

This is the background for our curriculum. It is a background steeped in The Great Conversation—the humility and grandeur of our existence—and it is a background that can both engage and vocationally prepare young inquirers.

Let us "play" a little, then, with a possible awe-based course sequence. There is nothing definitive about this proposal, and it is only provided as a stimulus for a more informed deliberative body. At the appropriate point in a student's career, say 4th grade through high school, an awe-based historical curriculum might focus on the following broad concerns: How do given cultures throughout history stifle or cultivate awe? How do those valences inform contemporary students? Again, awe is defined as the capacity for humility, reverence, and wonder: the thrill and anxiety of living. It is further defined as the realization of the delimiting and emboldening sides of living, not as separate poles but together as dialectical "wholes" of experience. In a nutshell, awe comprises a *dialectical* sensibility of discovery, adventure, and boldness melded to and in the context of safety, structure, and support. Awe mitigates against alienation (polarization)—either in the form of hyper-humility (humiliation) or hyper-boldness (arrogance).

Our proposed curriculum, then, opens in neolithic Europe and the Middle East. The first domain it would address is the shift from agrarian, goddess-based cultures to urban, warrior-based societies. For example, it might inform students about agrarian priorities such as relationships with the land, connection with nature, and devotion to community. It could illuminate humility and boldness in these eras and thereby their degree of fetishization, or what I will from now on refer to as "polarization." It might suggest, for example, that the land became an object of extreme reverence for these early peoples, that the trees, the lakes, and the mountaintops acquired god-like properties, and that the rains, the wind, and the changing of seasons appeared miraculous. This environmental adoration, however, may not have been matched by boldness of inquiry or intensity of imagination. The reverent and humbling sides of life appear to have outweighed those that were adventurous and wondering. The adoration paid to the Great Mother, the Creatrix of life, and the ritualized community may have also come at a price of suppressed individuality, stifled or neglected curiosity, and delimited growth. While many of these issues remain controversial, one point strikes clear: Students can acquire a wealth of insight from such historical anecdotes, and not just for their exams. Take the devotional relationship to nature among neolithic peoples—this alone could inspire a bevy of personal reflections, for example, concerning the role of nature in one's own life and the life of one's culture. Concerns about nature's spiritual and aesthetic importance and its impact on one's physical or mental health could all figure integrally into such a reflection. By the same token, many questions would arise regarding the potential drawbacks of agrarian and goddess-centered culture—such as the back-breaking work of a pre-industrial society, the concentration on pre-arranged familial and communal obligations, the injunctions against individual expression, and so on. In short, whole classes could be devoted to questions about polarization in agrarian and goddess cultures and the degree to which such polarization informs the student about his own relationships to nature, to manual labor, and to community.

Next, there could be explorations of the transition from neolithic culture to the modern city-state, as reflected, for example, by the ancient state of Israel. There could be evocative dialogues about the shift from pantheism to monotheism and from nomadic and matrilineal folkways to those of the agrarian and patrilineal. Students could explore the implications of this change for travel, establishment of property, militarism, and relationships. They could reflect on the consequences of the shift from the reverence for motherhood and earth to the worship of fatherhood and sky, the replacement of multiple deities by that of a central source, and the enlarged role of the individual. They could examine the polarities in the new paradigm, such as the accent on guilt, the yen for tribal conquest, and the preoccupation with national identity. They could also inquire into the ennobling and emancipatory aspects of the new worldview—such as the premium on cultural and individual independence, the eclipse, if not transcendence of idolatry, and the embrace of inter-ethnic tolerance.

The early Greek world of Homer and the pre-Socratics could also be edifying from an awe-based position. The transition from a bardic and mythic world, from the *Iliad* and the *Odyssey,* to a literary and philosophical world, a world of Sophocles, Plato and Aristotle, could be particularly instructive to students. In this regard, the clash between Dionysian (intuitive, expressive) and Appollonian (analytic, orderly) worldviews, and the implications of those worldviews for contemporary Western culture, would also be material. Essential to this aforementioned discussion would be the revolutionary Greek notions of freedom, democracy, the polis, and pride or hubris, as well as athleticism and cultivation of the body. Some of the contemporary questions one could raise about such material include: 1) What is the value of a mytho-poetic lifestyle? 2) Are we hurting over the absence of such a lifestyle in the post-industrial world? 3) What have we lost/gained by our linear and rational approach to life? 4) How could one integrate the early Greek concerns about courage, heroism, and hubris into one's own life? 5) What could one learn from the Greeks about balance and excess, fate and freedom, desire and foolishness?

In addition to raising questions about timely themes, such material could also inspire dances, dramatizations, songs, and mock forums. Further, there could be field trips to museums, films, and theatrical productions based on the curriculum. It is essential from this awe-based perspective that students not only reflect on and discuss the literature, but also, to the degree possible, experience, enact, and embody it.

The curriculum could also then move to the roots of Eastern culture—to the Indians, Chinese, Buddhists, Hindus, and Muslims. There could be forums on Indian asceticism and class consciousness, the cosmology of the Hindus, the "middle path" of the Buddhists, the dynastic successions of Chinese emperors, and the kinship rites of Islam. There could be rich debates about polarization/liberation in these worlds, their implications for the modern consciousness, and their relevance to individual lives.

This dialogue could be further vivified by a focus on modern versus traditional forms of Eastern worship. Among the issues confronted could be the role of an afterlife, fanaticism versus piety, and morality versus self-preservation.

In conjunction with the illumination of Eastern consciousness, we could also elucidate the awe-based folkways of historical Africa: the patchwork quilt of mystical, animistic, and ritualistic belief systems, the aesthetic and relational orientations, and the narratives that define the heritages. The legacy of ancient Egypt could also be plumbed—the majesty of the tombs, the grandeur of the pyramids, the splendor of the animal cults, and the wonder of the healing arts. By the same token, we could immerse students in the bewilderment of slavery, elitism, despotism, and human and animal sacrifice. Finally, we could elucidate Amenhotep IV, the lone pharaoh who anticipated the Judeo-Christian notion of monotheism.

Again, the questions here are how cultures have handled their anxieties and possibilities throughout history,[8] what we can learn from those labors, and how we can translate them for contemporary purposes. While it is obvious that there will be a degree of dissension about awe-based historical interpretations, these should not deter us. Entered in earnest, such a meditation will invariably evoke some degree of controversy. However, can inspired, energized, reflective people arrive at a consensus? Yes. Awe—the co-mingling of humility, reverence, and wonder—is a dimension that most people deeply prize, can exuberantly detect, and, if given the opportunity, will vigorously cultivate. Further, and as Becker has articulated in *Beyond alienation*, we are now at a stage in history where we can soundly—and with much hard-won realism—begin to evaluate such notions as awe. We can begin to reassess the tyrannies, autocracies, and oligarchies, the disempowering economies, and the oppressed and devitalized lifestyles that, in awe's absence, have thrived. By the same token, we can illuminate the "breaths of fresh air," the shining and ennobling moments, and the everyday human triumphs associated with awe's presence. Moreover, we are finally at a level of physical adaptation—and physical subsistence—where we can afford to ponder these ponderous problems and, indeed, we must!

The next logical sequence in our "awe" curriculum could be a critical analysis of ancient Rome. The focus here could be on the imperial aspirations of Roman leaders, the implementation of laws, and the treatment of diverse constituents. The forces of gloom and destruction and also those of radiance and innovation would be encountered through these studies. Students, for example, would learn about the tyrannous and arrogant overlords, but they would also discover the color, animation, and pageantry of the patriotic masses. They would learn of abject barbarism, and they would also witness breathless aestheticism—sculptures, monuments, and arenas. They would read of the wealth, stature, and privilege of Roman aristocrats, and they would also learn of the vapidity and desolation brought about by those attributes— the corrupting gluttony, savage jealousy, and merciless ennui. Students would also grapple with the lessons of imperial conquest, assimilation, and co-existence with autonomous cultures.

Then students would encounter the revolutionary teachings of Christ and the Christian oligarchy. They would explore both the legend and scholarly evidence about early Christian influences and critically evaluate New Testament declarations. They would grapple with Jesus' single-handed impact on Judaism and Roman imperialism, the implications of his egalitarian stand, and the institutionalization of that stand by founders of the Catholic church. They would look intimately at the question of idolatry, either as it was represented by Rome, the Jewish leadership, or the institutional church, and they would sift through the implications of such idolatry for elitism, scapegoating, and megalomania. They would also critically explore Christ's egalitarian challenge and its contemporary implications. They might be asked, for example, how the principle of love would play out at the level of international trade, distribution of resources, and religious partisanship? What would such a principle mean for one's personal identity, race and gender relations, and sense of ethics? These would be the burning tasks of scholarship.

The next phase of the curriculum could take students into the so-called Dark and Middle Ages of Europe. There could be illuminating dialogue about the medical and environmental conditions of the time, the onslaught of the bubonic plague, and the relationships between serfs, feudal lords and the church. Many intriguing questions could be raised about the neglect of sanitary conditions, the life of indentured servitude, and the airy stature of nobility. Equally, however, there could be a wealth of investigation into the devotional aspects of medieval life—the impact of the papacy, the resistance to Roman and Greek classicism, the respect for duty, service, and national patronage. Yet above and beyond these influences, there could be a particular focus on the all-consuming devotion to God. According to theorists as varied as Marx and Becker, it is this devotion that differentiated feudal life from many other class-based communities. Although many societies accented material gain, for better or worse, the feudal fiefdoms of Europe prioritized religiosity. To explore expressions of this religiosity—from the brick-laying of cathedrals to the devotional vows of knighthood to the blood-orgies of inquisitors—would be the core of a multi-faceted dialogue.

The next elucidating sequence in our awe-curriculum would be the Renaissance. Named for "rebirth," this dynamic and revitalizing period poses a variety of social and philosophical challenges that remain today. For example, students could explore the revival of Greek humanism—in Renaissance terms, the *studia humanitatis*—in light of the theism that preceded it. They could especially home in on the parallels between the growing needs for industrialization in the Renaissance era and the advent of rationalism, the rise of the mercantile class, innovations in travel, the emergence of religious alienation, and the quest for self-expression. Fascinating dilemmas could be posed about the costs of these new developments—the loss of theistic purpose and religious identity, the erosion of craftsmanship, and the diminishment of service and duty to the crown. On the other hand, students could reflect abundantly about the benefits of the era: for example, the newfound freedoms, technical developments, and expansions of literacy. Students could also explore humanity's rejuvenated belief in itself—its capacity for innovation, artistic achievement, and physical fulfillment. Conversely, they could grapple with the limitations of these developments: the confinement of humanism to worldly rather than transcendent ends, the arrogance as well as devitalization that can associate with such a position, and the breakdown of community, ritual, and authority.

The next logical sequence would examine the emergence of the Enlightenment and the flowering of science. This portion would delve into the nature, role, and impact of science on daily life. Students would explore how discoveries in physics, astronomy, physiology and the like affected standards of living, work life, and interpersonal relations. They would translate that understanding into their current situations. In particular, they would consider how systematic observation, rational argumentation, and technical proficiency promote or detract from the cultivation of awe—i.e., whether scientific procedures stifle or enhance one's capacity for inquiry, discovery, and life purpose. The Reformation, the liberation and subsequent terror in France, and the advent of Romanticism, would each be critically considered. Questions would be raised about the pros and cons of the Reformation as a reaction to papal autocracy, the French Revolution as a counter to privilege and monarchy, and Romanticism as a response to arid technocracy.

Next students would reflect on the intricacies of religious rebellion in England and the advent of the American Revolution. They would investigate the Protestant offshoots of Puritanism, Calvinism, and Lutheranism, and their values. They would survey the Quaker, Amish, and Mormon struggles, and they would grapple with early colonial life. In particular, they would look at the implications of that life for work, relationships, nature, and politics. They would compare and contrast the colonial folkways with those of Native Americans and raise hard questions about subsistence, standards of living, educational practices, community, and environment. They would also examine the spiritual and ethical beliefs of the respective nationalities, and they would consider all the dimensions for their personal and contemporary import.

Here, as in all areas of history, no view would go unchallenged; no coherent stance would be barred. Next there would be a frank encounter with the colonial and post-colonial perspective on slavery. There would be challenging dialogues on the role, nature, and consequences of "owning" human beings. In particular, students would wrestle with the dynamics that led to the slavery of Africans, the impact of coercion, for both slave and master, and the legacy of a "slave culture." At the same time, students would grapple with the dignity, resiliency, and community that managed to arise among some slaves, in spite of their torments. The whole question of "in spite of"—faith in spite of doubt, meaning in spite of absurdity, and hope in spite of despair—would be deliberated.

The heroic actions of former slaves such as Frederick Douglass, and liberators such as Nat Turner and Abraham Lincoln, would also be elucidated. The questions of courage and of looking beyond self-interest would be an integral part of the dialogue regarding these prominent figures. Further, the issues of manifest destiny and of absolutist beliefs would be encountered. The ambiguity of those positions, their power to crush and exalt, would be examined.

The "conquest" of the western United States, the domination of nature, and the wizardry of technical innovation would also be explored. The price as well as benefit of these developments would be scrutinized and related to current problems. The treatment of laborers, immigrants, and women would all be probed, as would the aggrandizement of "old boys' networks," "blue-bloods," and "barons of industry." The capitalist dream of material acquisition, Machiavellian power, and individual interest would be counterposed by discussions about utopian ideals, such as labor movements, struggles for civil rights, and egalitarianism. Some of the relevant questions for students within this context would be: How did America and much of the Western world fall into these predicaments? What remedies, with how much success, were employed to address them?

Finally, students would be immersed in the sobering and dramatic twentieth century, with its techno-wizardry and crimes of inhumanity. They will begin their study with the hopeful period pre-dating World War I, as well as its shattering aftermath at the Austro-Hungarian border. Students will shudder before the expansionist ambitions of the Austro-Hungarian empire, as well as the post-World War I designs of America and Western Europe. They will toil with the rise of Japanese nationalism and the fall of British imperialism, the surge in Western wealth, and the crash in Western markets. They will plunge neck-deep into the tragedy at Versailles, the isolationist drift of the American leaders, the impotency of the League of Nations, and the enthrallment of Nazi hate. They will wade into the intensifying tide of fascism: from Italy to Spain, from Germany to East Europe, and from the American

Bund movement to the Japanese imperial empire. They will witness hate and the dissemination of hate as they had never previously existed. Us versus Them, fetishization, and scapegoating will all be vivified in this dialogue: The torment of the Jews and other Holocaust victims will be the central, tragic illustration.

Next, students would range over the introduction of the atomic bomb and the Cold War, the implications of the potential for global destruction, and the consolidation of *realpolitik*. The conservatism of the 1950s and the liberalism of the 1960s will each receive their turn. African-American civil rights and the sexual, moral, and cultural revolutions of Europe and America will be scrutinized, as will the Sovietization of East Europe and the hegemonic ambitions in communist China. The core concern here will be discovery: What can we learn from the excesses of the twentieth century? What part of awe was neglected in these indulgences? What part affirmed? For example, how can the release of nuclear energy associate with the thrill, uplift, and betterment of humankind, rather than merely its debasement? How can conservatism connect with dynamism as much as it does with routinization? How can liberalism link up with commitment, consistency, and clarity as much as it does with frivolity, unruliness, and obscurity?

Finally, students would encounter the landmarks of the late twentieth-century, particularly as they are understood in the West. These would include the end of the Cold War, the rise of tribalism, the increasing tensions with Islamic fundamentalism, Christian and Jewish orthodoxy, and spiritual vacuity. At the same time, they will examine the explosion of information technology and the mind-bending revolutions in medicine, biotechnology, and evolutionary science. They will ponder the wonders of genetic engineering and the engineering of new species. They will stammer before the latest insights of ecology, climatology, physics, and astronomy, and they will tussle with the computer revolution, the internet, and telecommuting. They will explore the New Age and communitarian movements, the revival of paganism, and the diversification of religiosity. They will square off with the resurgence in right wing extremism—militias, neo-Nazism, and white supremacy movements. And finally, they will plunge into the brave new world of global markets and global terror. To all of this, they will awaken and massage into values.

The net effect of the awe curriculum would be to challenge students to prioritize: not to prioritize in empty or mechanized routines, but to prioritize richly, roundly, and energetically—to prioritize with intentionality. By intentionality, I mean a prioritization that evolves from struggle, play, and discovery and that, as a result, aligns with one's innermost core, one's maximal embodiment, one's entire spirit. This is the kind of prioritization that one throws one's whole being into and that animates the hours. This, of course, is the ideal, but we could come a lot closer to it if awe were cultivated as we now cultivate "competency."

The cultivation of competency, however, would not be lost in this animating curriculum. Core competencies in math, science, English, and the like would all be included in the awe curriculum; they would not be taught in isolation, removed from their real-world contexts. And this approach would become particularly necessary for primary and secondary school students, before they become shunted into specialties or careers. In this curriculum, students would encounter the vast tapestry of inquiry—of play and experimentation, reflection and dialogue, and real-life concerns and application—upon which one's competencies are drawn. And there is plenty to draw upon and plenty of befuddlement about the absence of such a direction in contemporary education.

For example, one educator, Wyn Wachhorst,[9] asks: "why…are schools almost bereft of students who sense the larger dimensions of science?… In a universe immense and mysterious beyond imagining," he continues, "why do so many of our youth wallow in world-weary ignorance?" (p. 36). Wachhorst then goes on to tell his own story about growing up in the 1940s and 1950s in Palo Alto, California. He cites his "old Uncle George" as the catalyst to measureless moments of joy as his Uncle waxed rhapsodically about the fantastic. "One night, " Wachhorst reports, "he told me about the canals on Mars. They might have been built, he said, by an older, wiser civilization heroically trying to delay extinction. It was a wondrous image, a fire in a small boy's mind" (p. 35).

One morning under his family's Christmas tree, Wachhorst elaborates, "I found a book of astronomical paintings."

> In it were silver ships poised needle-nosed on the craggy wastes of other worlds, alien moonscapes bathed in the stark light of some monster planet, and of course, the rocky green hills of Mars, rolling like the coast of Maine along the great canals, looking over a far desert where ruins stood half in sand. I cut out the pages and communed with the pictures, enshrined on my walls (p. 35).

Finally, Wachhorst goes on to describe how as a teenager he "drank in" a low-budget, science fiction thriller and concludes: "From my first real encounter with the cosmos, waking one night at summer camp under a soul-searching canopy of stars, to the day, a half century later, when *Pathfinder* put its rover on the red desert of the real Mars, my deep sense of wonder has owed a great debt to a cracker-barrel story, a mistaken book, and a bad movie" (p. 36).

Contemporaneous with the awe-based historical curriculum, then, we would offer awe-based curricula in science, math, literature, social studies, physical education, the arts, and socialization. As Wachhorst suggests, the key is the seedbed, the immersion in "the great mysteries—things strange beyond comprehension—immensities beyond imagination" (p. 38)—and then specialization in that which practically applies or narrows one's field. The value of such a direction—both for individuals and the culture at large—cannot be overstated. Let us look more closely at why this is so.

If a science curriculum, for example, were to begin with the marvels, if films, books, and inspiring stories were used as stimuli, if field trips were the norm, think how much more exuberance students would bring to their studies and to their lives.

There are several basic qualities that such a curriculum, or any awe-based sequence, would help students to clarify: First, it would teach them how to better treat themselves. Second, it would teach them how to better treat our world. Third, it would give them an enhanced appreciation of human freedom—which is implied though not entirely exhausted by the above two insights. The course sequence would teach them to better treat themselves because it would be rife with examples of such treatment. It would be rife with anecdotes about self-hate, deprivation, and indignation and, at the same time, brimming with lessons about self-love, hope, and affirmation. It would show how the Greeks treated themselves when they focused on philosophy and the life of the polis; and equally, when they homed in on war and imperial ambition. It would show how slaves reacted under the aegis of captivity and how they responded to freedom, democracy, and self-initiative. It would illuminate the personal experiences of agrarians and those of urban dwellers, of worshipers and of secularists, of romanticists and of rationalists, and of inquirers and followers. It would highlight the exhilaration of sport and contest and the destitution of war and tyranny. It would examine the experience of healing and healing relationships and it would unveil depravity and suffering.

It would teach students how to better treat the world through the example of the historical treatment of the world. This treatment would include relations between factions, cultures, and races. But, equally, it would examine peoples' connection with nature, the planet, and the cosmos itself. It would illuminate oppressive interrelations as well as those that invigorate and inspire. And it would highlight dynamic ranges between these polarities. Finally, the awe curriculum would teach students about freedom and the cost of freedom. In particular, it would help students to identify those eras and cultures that "speak to" current struggles with liberation, as well as the limits of those struggles. How, for example, might the ancient Greek notion of hubris illuminate the contemporary challenges of genetic engineering, computerized warfare, and medicalized mental health? What can the aristocrats of Rome clarify about self-indulgence, arrogance, and class consciousness? How does the Renaissance elucidate artistic freedom, personal expression, and the limits of reason; or Romanticism, the thresholds of caprice? What can indigenous Africans teach about embodied ritual, or

Asians about engaged non-attachment? What can any era or culture inform students about global emancipation?

These are the burning questions that students would bring to their specialties and that would lead them to fuller, more fervent vocations.

Back to our science curriculum—how much more students could bring to anatomy, physiology, astronomy, physics, and the like, if only they combined awe with their studies. Take a student of astronomy. Not only would such a student know the locations, movements, and conditions of planets, he would also know something of how planets have been perceived throughout history in religious treatises and in fictional, classic narratives. He would have access to a spirit of discovery, mystery, and possibility, as well as to formulae, instruments, and tests. What would these dimensions add? The answer is both clear and speculative. The clear answer is that an awe-based astronomical education would bring a wealth of affective, intuitive, and philosophical appreciation that our current competency-based programs just could not muster. While the competency-based programs help students to perceive fine numerical distinctions and overt occurrences, the awe-based background would supply something radically different—the "experience" of astronomical phenomena. The experience of astronomical phenomena may include, but is not exhausted by, the gleeful reminiscence of sky-watching; the detection of chills or thrills during routine telescopic surveys; the radical openness to diverse theoretical models; the yen for adventure, innovation, and the extraordinary; the resonance with fellow sky-watchers, whether of scientific or poetic inclination; and the passion for hunches, hypotheses, and imaginative visions.

Less clear, on the other hand, would be the impact of an awe-based astronomical background on basic or applied research. My wager, however, is that such an education would associate with actual, technical advancement. If Einstein, Newton, Descartes, Poincaré, and other leading scientists are any indication, then the holistic attunement to life, which includes dreams, intuitions, and inspirational visions, is integral to discovery. Moreover, it is integral to the motivation to discover.

Beyond the question of technical advance, however, is the question of quality of life. Awe brings zest, angst, and passion to the inquiry process; it brings *the capacity to be moved.* With this capacity, experimentation becomes an excursion and verification a touchstone. Who knows what groups of moved scientists could offer to the world or to each other? In any case, like Wachhorst's little boy, they would be intensively engaged.

Consider further what awe would bring to the careers of geneticists, physicians, and mental health providers. Consider how humility and boldness, reverence and wonder would color their work. In all likelihood, for example, the awe-informed geneticist would be deeply reflective about the use of his data. He would treat the implications of his data with foresight and sensitivity, not merely dispassion. In all likelihood, he would view genes and behavior as complex, integrative systems, and he would resist efforts to downplay or deny that intricacy. Dogma, puritanism, and political manipulation would also be of concern to this astute individual, as would extremes of any kind. In as much as he would be ethically attuned, he is likely to welcome others—such as philosophers, psychologists, concerned laypersons—into dialogue about issues of concern. In short, the awe-informed geneticist is likely to neither deny nor promote zealously problematic research, but to act with wonder and discernment.

An awe-informed physician would be an intensely fresh breeze for many in the medical world. Such a physician would have a sense of her impact on the lives of her clients, as well as on that of her co-workers. She would detect and grapple with her own reactions to the anguish and profundity of her task, and she would enable the communication of such concerns by others. She would recognize the degree to which medicine is emotionally loaded and how centrally that loading affects treatment. Time and emotional availability would be integral aspects of her approach with clients, as would an inquiring spirit tempered by concreteness and practicality. A collaborative and holistic approach would be prioritized, and in the context of the former, the use of state-of-the-art technology. The physician would regularly consult with allied practitioners—psychologists, clergy, nutritionists—and she would routinely encourage patients to educate themselves about such services. Love, freedom, and fear would all be normative topics for discussion in these settings—and so would the meaning and implications of the illness for patients' lives. In all likelihood, there would be many more students willing to be trained as healers within this holistic context and, hence, many more opportunities for patients to consult with and substantively engage their practitioners. Money would be less of an obstacle as well for, as mentioned earlier, all mental and physical health services could be federally and privately subsidized—and physicians (as with all socially critical service providers) would make reasonable and viable salaries.

Mental health providers would occupy a much more central role in the awe-based culture. The reason for this—notwithstanding my own biases as a practicing therapist—is that the cultivation of aliveness, of depth, and of maximal access to experience would be crucial grist for the mill in every major human endeavor. We have already looked at the cultivation of these aspects in the work, educational, and medical settings, but it would be of equal pertinence in the contexts of marriage, romantic relationships, families, religious affiliations, and professional and recreational organizations. Simply put, an awe-based culture would demand the active and widely available services of expert facilitators of emancipation.[10] The other side of this proposition is that the mental health providers would only tangentially reflect the current cadre of such service providers. These new providers will be schooled, not merely in the voguish techniques of cognitive and biological science, but also in the holistic, philosophical, and humanitarian modalities of anthropological science. These new service providers, in other words, will be more like doctors of souls than doctors of isolated minds, or bodies, or behaviors. They will be facilitators of the thoughts, feelings, and intuitions that underlie the overt words or mannerisms, and they will help bring those underlying potentialities into practical realization. These facilitators, moreover, will emphasize qualitative dimensions of human experience over those which are statistically aggregated. They will draw upon subtly nuanced, rigorously performed qualitative investigations of life to arbitrate and help guide their practices. The composition of these new healers, finally, will be diverse—psychologists, psychiatrists, anthropologists, clergy, holistic healers, and philosophers—but their training would meet rigorous, mutually agreed upon standards of service.[11]

Next, let us consider a student of a very different persuasion—the building trade: How might awe play out in her development? While the aforementioned question may at first blush seem strange or even bizarre, it is hardly thus. Our hypothesized student, for example, would bring to her skills as a builder a deep appreciation for nature, a critical understanding of how nature has been devalued, and an aesthetic awareness of what about nature inspires. At the same time, this student would not be naïve about nature. She would learn indelibly of nature's fury, threat, and perceived brutality. She would discover humanity's intensive need to protect itself from and co-exist with nature. She would bring all this to her mapping of a high-rise or grasp of a cross-beam. Further, she would bring an awareness of the social inequities in construction and of the tendencies to ignore or short-change poorer consumers. She would know of the inhumanities among fellow workers and the implications of these for the culture at large. The tendencies to cut co-workers off, or to treat them as instruments, categories, or stereotypes, would all be accounted for by her and by the system she allows herself to work within.

The upshot of these examples is that they are but a few of the literally millions that could be considered. Ponder the effect of an entire nation of awe-informed citizenry, for example, or an awe-informed workforce. They would pour into businesses and specialties of every stripe, armed with an appreciation for life—an appreciation for existence—that would radically transform culture. Consider again the impact of such an education for the atmosphere of the work-place. We've already touched on some of the alterations implied, such as mental and physical well-being activities, group process meetings, and empowerment within the workplace. But what of all the subtle aspects of this background—the elevations of mood, energy, physical and mental health, motivation for the job, sense of freedom to imagine and create and to collaborate with co-workers? What of the freedom to simply "be," if that is what is needed for a period, or to get to know and become friends/allies with those in one's industry? Or, on the other hand, what of the opportunity to grapple with conflicts with co-workers in the relative safety of professionally led groups or therapeutic settings? All of these possibilities and more would be available in the revolutionary new work space of humility and boldness, respect and autonomy.

As for the new domestic and social spaces affected by the awe-based frame, this, too, would transform. Consider the working mom who has time for her children or the stay-at-home dad who feels nourished by both work and family. Consider the enrichment of the children who are impacted by such dispositions—the love, guidance, and validation they would receive. Consider the enrichment of relationships generally when relatively fulfilled and aware people interact with one another—the spirit that is shared, the substantive issues that are explored, and the accessibility that is offered.

Finally, what of the impact of an awe-informed education on the government, the military, and even the presidency? It is almost too auspicious to imagine—but let us try anyway. Consider, for example, the humility, discernment, and understanding offered by an awe-informed state senator. He would be a person who has grappled with hubris, with the dynamics of greed, and with the vicissitudes of hate, lust and fear—and not just in history books, but among people he knows, and in his own breast. Consider a governor who has studied *Beloved, When the Cage Bird Sings,* and *Hamlet*. Think about a president who has been immersed in philosophy, great myths, and the wisdom-teachings of religion. Reflect upon a general who has absorbed Plato's *Dialogues, Tao Te Ching* and *The Death of Ivan Ilych,* as well as Thucydides's *Histories* and *The Rise and Fall of the Third Reich.* All these dimensions and more would be brought to the awe-informed political arena. All these attunements to humanity's estrangements and debasements, as well as its nourishments and ennoblements, would be deliberated upon.

6

Tragedy and Its Ambiguities: Awe and Its Paradoxes

Her work is acid and tender;
Hard as steel and fine as a butterfly's wing;
Lovable as a smile;
Cruel as the bitterness of life.
I don't believe that ever before has a woman put such
agonized poetry on canvas.

—Diego Rivera (Alfred Molina) speaking about his wife, Frida Kahlo
(Salma Hayek) in the film, *Frida*, 2002, Miramax Productions

Despite the magnificent possibilities of an awe-based life, there are also terrible realities to this and every other kind of life. And they must not be skirted. These realities comprise the human condition, the condition of all life on our planet. Life appears and it withers away. It bursts out in spring-like glory and it implodes, shatters, and scatters to the winds.

Tragedy is as integral to awe as awe is to life. Even in an awe-informed world, there will be murders, rapes, and debasements. There will be bigotry and poverty, and tyranny will ever be a specter. Among people, there will ever be an element of the pernicious. Although there is likely to be less human-created mayhem in an awe-infused society, inhumanity and its taproot, fear, are not likely to be stanched. Moreover, nature-created catastrophe will proceed unabated. There will inevitably be death, disease, and natural destruction. There will unavoidably be hurricanes and earthquakes, bloody bodies removed from landfalls, supernovae and dwarf stars, and the withering of all matter.

Ultimately, therefore, there will inexorably be a "condition" within which all must dwell. While this condition may have many names and formulations, it appears to possess a common core: unmanageability, groundlessness, or the dimension that Tillich terms "nonbeing."[1] Nonbeing, according to Tillich, is that portion of "being" that so radically deviates from our common sensibilities, our common understanding, that it is perceived as annihilating. Put another way, nonbeing is the *mysterium tremendum,* the holy of holies, and the unspeakable of biblical lore.[2] While nonbeing can certainly refer to literal death, it more often connotes the *mystery* of death, the mystery of that which exceeds human apprehension. Nonbeing therefore bewilders, confuses, and terrifies. It also polarizes—and to the extent that this polarization becomes extreme, it can lead to its own terror, confusion, and bewilderment. In either case, as Tillich notes, nonbeing can be understood in terms of two basic "nightmares:"

> "The one type is the anxiety of annihilating narrowness, of the impossibility of escape and the horror of being trapped [e.g., the terrors of despair, powerlessness, and debilitation]. The other is the anxiety of annihilating openness, of infinite, formless space into which one falls without a place to fall upon [e.g., the torments of disarray, derangement, and anarchy]."

Both nightmares, concludes Tillich, "arouse the latent anxiety [and I might add 'defensiveness'] of every individual who looks at them."[3]

Yet Tillich suggests another perspective on nonbeing that is not nearly so dour.[4] At the same time that nonbeing is mortifying, it is also potentially liberating; it is the doorway to new relationships, new realizations, and new strengths. If only we had the courage, Tillich asserts, if only we could confront, absorb, grapple with the polarities of our nightmares, then we could live more engaged and poignant lives—we could live with fuller access to our lives. Here, Tillich echoes Rilke: "We must assume our existence as *broadly* as we in any way can; everything, even the unheard of, must be possible in it. That is at bottom the only courage demanded of us: to have courage for the most strange, the most

singular and the most inexplicable that we may encounter."[5] Ditto
Pascal: "For after all, what is man in nature? A nothing in regard
to the infinite, a whole in regard to nothing, a mean between
nothing and the whole; infinitely removed from understanding
either extreme....What shall [we] do then but discern somewhat
of the middle of things....We are something, but we are not all."[6]

Let us grant then that the chaos and obliteration of the universe mirrors not just the heart of human dread, but also, with
equal vehemence, the heart of human possibility.

To whom or what would an awe-based society turn to cultivate the latter? Is there a fluid center of tragedy?

The answer is as invigorating as it is obvious—an awe-informed world would turn for illumination to its own awe-leavened
legacy, its own storehouse of myth, art, and ministry, and its own
finely tuned sensibilities. These sensibilities are key to the entire
awe-based corpus, the entire fluidly centered world. We have repeatedly alluded to these sensibilities, but let us spell them out
boldly now: they are ambiguity and paradox—the ambiguous and
the paradoxical. Now these qualities, it should be underscored, are
not in the least prosaic. They do not refer merely to open-mind-
edness, "flexible thinking," or pluralism. By contrast, they refer to
the most supple and yet neglected of human perceptual capacities,
and they are at the core of all awe-based depictions of vitality. The
cultivation of the ambiguous and paradoxical, then, can be understood as the cultivation of the acceptance of and encounter with
contrasting polarities of experience. Correspondingly, to the extent
that one can engage in this cultivation, one experiences a resultant
deepening, sharpening, and enlargement.[7] As may be evident, the
cultivation of ambiguity and paradox directly parallels the cultivation of awe: It is the stark realization of our dialectical nature—our
miniscule yet colossal nature—before creation. Out of this realization, vivid illumination can occur.[8]

To grasp the difference between the ambiguous/paradoxical
and the pluralistic/anarchic life-orientations, consider the role of
struggle. Whereas anarchism and pluralism suggest a helter-skel-
ter, "anything goes" experience, the ambiguous and paradoxical

ever imply an "incubation" or immersion in experience. The difference here is profound—for whereas anarchism and pluralism
can (and have) led to a kind of cult of caprice, the centrifugal
forces of ambiguity and paradox resist such polarizing.[9] From the
perspective of the ambiguous and paradoxical, in other words,
the moment one polarizes (fixates, fetishizes)—even if that polarizing is expansive—one blocks the contrasting element (e.g.,
constriction), which almost invariably beckons.[10] In crude terms,
the ambiguous and paradoxical "keep us honest"—they shy neither from humanity's meagerness nor its magnificence—and, in
so doing, they foster wisdom.

But it is one thing to report on these fine points, it is quite
another to experience them directly or through the eloquence of
art. Let us return to our opening reflection on the myths, artistry,
and ministry that inform the awed.

The Greek myth of Sisyphus is an example par excellence of
an awe-leavened response to tragedy. Condemned by Zeus to roll
a rock up a hill for all eternity, only to have it roll back down again
and have to repeat the process, indefinitely, Sisyphus is a distressed
soul. Yet Sisyphus has a secret, as the philosopher Albert Camus
informs us: despite his duress, he is "happy."[11] Why?—because he
discovers choice, will, and even passion in his laborious task, *in his
approach to his task*. For example, he finds zest in setting shoul-
der to rock, tasting sweat dripping from his face, planting feet at
just the desired angle, and breathing air, sweetened by mountain
flora. In short, Sisyphus finds solace in the most objectionable
circumstances by plunging himself into those circumstances and
by sopping up their every facet—and so, encouragingly, could we,
suggests the parable, if only we could tap the paradoxical.

Interestingly, it is precisely this engagement with choice that
fuels Victor Frankl's meditations on Nazi concentration camps.[12]
There are ways to perceive possibilities, he conveys, even in the most
depraved of conditions. Further, it is precisely by acknowledging
the depravity of the circumstances that the response to them may
be heightened, the morsels of hope, freedom, and life within them
concentrated. "Verse, fame, and beauty, are intense indeed," writes

Keats, "But death intenser—Death is life's high mead."[13]

While there are a wealth of illustrations of awe-informed responses to tragedy—Sophocles' *Oedipus,* Dante's *Inferno,* Goethe's *Faust,* Shakespeare's *Hamlet,* Tolstoy's *Ilych,* not to mention the Old and New Testaments—the example of the horror tale has been oddly neglected in literary and psychological quarters.[14] Yet, as I suggested earlier, the paradigm of classic horror is integral to an awe-informed meditation on tragedy. Classic horror and suspense, in particular, take us to the furthest horizons of human dread, but they also direct us to the peak of human hopes, dreams, and desires, alongside of that dread.[15] It is in this light, then, that our awe-based culture should turn, not just to conventional fiction, but to the haunting yarn for its emotional sustenance; for it is this genre as much or even more than other classic genres that transports us to the very core of our humanity, the very crux of our quest.

Hidden Treasures of "Horror": Classic Horror as Awe-Based Illumination

Whereas I previously addressed the significance of classic horror for traumatized individuals, I will now consider its implications for society. What can horror tales inform us about the moral and ethical problems of society, and how can this understanding transform individual lives?

As noted previously, the foundation of classic horror is the double or doppelganger. The double invokes our smallness and greatness, our insignificance as well as our magnificence before creation. To the extent that these tensions can only be "pointed to" or suggested, rather than literally portrayed, the literature that addresses them also must point to or suggest. Classic horror performs precisely this task, and it does so at a variety of personal and social levels. It is important, therefore, to dwell deeply on these stories and to consider their many-sided lessons. Robert Louis Stevenson's *The Strange Case of Dr. Jekyll and Mr. Hyde,* is a case in point. In this challenging drama, Dr. Jekyll's tragedy is also, by implication, his salvation, illumination, and liberation. Although these breakthroughs are rarely explicated in either the text or film versions of the story, they are strongly intimated by a series of critical junctures. The first juncture is Jekyll's repressed Victorian nature. There is a strong tone of suffering in this nature, particularly in the superlative 1932 film adaptation of the story. In that adaptation, Jekyll continually berates himself and his culture for "holding back," checking impulses, and quashing feelings. He presses for his girlfriend's hand in marriage but is repeatedly rebuked by her father. He dreams of social and psychological emancipation and yet he is perpetually admonished for entertaining them by his colleague, Lanyon. The net effect of these frustrations is to vividly bring to our attention their tragic validity particularly in the Western world and, by implication, to suggest means and methods by which they may be alleviated. The alleviation that Jekyll discovers, of course, is to become Hyde, which forms the second critical juncture. By becoming Hyde, Jekyll goes far beyond that which could arguably be viewed as liberating and transforms into a mockery of his vision. Yet it is precisely this mockery, this extreme, that becomes so pivotal from the standpoint of awe. It is precisely in Hyde's exaggerated movements—his leaps and spins and shifts of direction—his impetuosity, his boorishness, his caprice, and even his tyrannical fury that the exhilarating and emancipating possibilities in Jekyll become evident. Hyde becomes a metaphor. He contains the best and worst of what Jekyll and, by implication, everyperson can be: bold, erotic, spontaneous, and imaginative. But he can only be a metaphor from this awe-based standpoint; he cannot realistically replace Jekyll. To replace Jekyll is to replace the flesh and blood and woundedness of who we are and what we humanly face. Only Jekyll *and* Hyde—Hyde facing Jekyll and Jekyll facing Hyde—can join together the elements that enlarge human consciousness and provide hope for our future. Summing up, then, both Jekyll and Hyde in isolation are tragedies. Jekyll is a tragedy of devitalization and Hyde of vital overload. It is only by encountering these polarities, Stevenson intimates, that a new person and a greatly dilated range can genuinely emerge.

Mary Shelley's *Frankenstein* is one of the great doppelganger novels of the past 200 years. The wonderment of a scientist—an investigator of the noblest rank, stretched between his despair at the loss of his mother and his deranged creation—is a fertile problem, indeed. Whereas *Jekyll and Hyde* plumbs the tragedies of repression and conformity, *Frankenstein* plumbs the embattlements of despair, impotency, and fanaticism.

After some sublime foreshadowing, *Frankenstein* opens in a modest upper class household nestled in a beatific Swiss woods. Victor Frankenstein, the tale's protagonist, is a chipper youth raised among caring and supportive parents and a loving step-sister, Elizabeth. All appears to be favorable until a sudden and harrowing fever seizes Elizabeth. After much suffering, she survives the ordeal, but only because Frankenstein's loving mother aids her, but she then dies herself. The impression left by this shocking episode upon the youthful Victor was enormous. Within several years, he not only immerses himself in the study of medicine, but he also plunges into the study of the re-animation of life!

The story, as many are aware, leads to a tormenting conclusion—a corpse-created monster, a line of unsuspecting casualties of the monster's vengefulness, and the lament-filled demise of Victor himself on a lonely Nordic sea. But from the awe-based standpoint, it is the subtleties of this story that illuminate, and to these we now turn. One of the chief teachings of *Frankenstein* is neither that Victor was an incautious narcissist who relentlessly pursued his perverted fantasies, nor that in the wake of his pursuits, he and Elizabeth lost the opportunity for an ordinary and settled life together. It is both these aspects and, in particular, that which resides *between* them that is key. What I mean here is that the significance of *Frankenstein* dwells in the astonishing energy between his fanatical quest to extend life and the humiliation and impotency of his tragic ordeal. The magic of this tale, in other words, is its inquiry into response-ability versus reactivity, or ambiguous perceiving versus polarized perceiving. To the extent that

Frankenstein could have grappled with his mother's horrifying demise and absorbed its attendant turmoil, he potentially could have pursued both his recovery and ambitions. The ambitions, however, would not likely have evolved as they did in the story. There are several reasons for this contention. First, to the extent that he engaged his recovery, he would not, in all likelihood, be as desperate to thwart death as he was in the story. Second, given his more acceptant state, he would more likely be deliberative about his studies, considering their implications from many angles, and methodically advancing his work. Third, he would more likely be attentive to Elizabeth and to those in his life who had immediate significance to him—such as the loved ones in his life and possibly even the community and humanity that surrounded him. In short, he would be likely to appreciate the amazement of both life and death, resiliency and fragility, in all future endeavors. And what of the monster, the inventor's crowning "achievement?" This is a many-faceted question. While it is clear that a more tempered, more centered Frankenstein would seek to avoid the fate of his literary creation, would he avert revolutionary studies? Would he demur at electrifying nerve endings and repairing broken body parts, or even restoring dead tissue? These are not simple questions and the awe-based response to them is inconclusive. There are no purities or "happily ever afters" in this awe-based scenario. The novel provides us with no risk-free "solutions." Still, it is tempting to believe that, like his marvel-struck rescuer, Walton, a more awe-centered Frankenstein, would indeed maintain his innovative zeal—albeit with greater safeguards. He would transform his "monster" into a "monster" project or "monster" invention in the positive sense, and his methodology to that end would become healing rather than divisive. An analogous example might be the restriction of gene therapy to the alleviation of physical ailments versus personal or collective whim, or the limiting of robotic technology to information-giving versus decision-making.

The questions that classic horror pose then are how will one respond to the tragic (in Frankenstein's case, the death of his mother) and what opportunities/perils does that response present? In the case of Frankenstein, as with many horror protagonists the response was a blind and fanatical reaction, a "monstrosity" both literally and figuratively. But we know from depth psychology that such a reaction is not at all inexorable, and indeed the novel adroitly reminds us why. Recall that in the opening scene, a haunted and exasperated Frankenstein shows up on the deck of an expeditionary ship in the North Sea. The captain of the ship, Robert Walton, sits down with him to hear his story. His greatest woe, Frankenstein conveys, is his own bullheaded drivenness, his own obsessiveness, his own obliviousness to life. Hence Frankenstein's chief tragedy is his own string of omissions. First, he omitted to mourn and contemplate the death of his mother, then he omitted to consider the consequences of his death-defying defense against this death, then he omitted to share his anguish and seek counsel from his loved ones, and, finally, he omitted to care for and nurture his own creation. Each step of the way, in other words, Frankenstein omitted to pause over his endeavors; he omitted to grapple with ambivalent and contradictory parts of himself; and as a result, he dashed what many of us would call his humanity—his ability to discern.

The tragedy in Bram Stoker's *Dracula* is vengeance. While the persona of Dracula is treacherous, menacing, and hate-filled, the symbolism or intimation of his character is far more complex. Few people recall that Dracula was once a flesh and blood count, a leader and defender of his people who became embroiled in a blood-feud. The battle pitted his native peoples, the Huns, against their centuries-old adversaries, the Turks. In a desperate struggle with his Turk attackers, Dracula, along with legions of his countrymen, were butchered, enslaved, and desecrated. Before he died, however, Dracula vowed eternal vengeance against this atrocity, and from then on he became a warrior of the underworld, a servant of the "undead."

In his transformation from infuriated mortal to vengeful ghoul, Dracula echoes a classic trajectory—from victim to perpetrator to victim. While the torments of this trajectory are well known,[16] its potential salutary aspects are less appreciated. Dracula introduces us to a hidden world—a world of death, decay, and offense, to be sure, but also a world of subtlety, style, and seduction. In this world, Dracula finds within himself all means of physical and psychological resiliency—all means of cunning, cleverness, and metaphysical strength. He can command the beasts ("creatures of the night"), read minds, appear and disappear at will, contract himself into a shadow, and flail about with the force of ten men. He is mesmerizing to the core, and he overtakes his victims with a glance. His glare is incendiary and his agility breathtaking. Women, in particular, are susceptible to his maneuvers—and it is no wonder! There is a certain androgyny about Dracula, a certain yin to most men's yang that holds a particular allure for women. He calls to them without voice, stirs them without touch, denudes them without inquiry, and ravages them without sign or memory. Dracula is in some ways like the perfect underworld lover—ripe for dreams and fantasies. He is the unconscious incarnate. For men, too, he is captivating—both laser-like and ruthless.

Just how Dracula acquired such super-human abilities is never told. What is told, however, is enough to point us in certain directions. As an ancient count at the time of his mortal life (roughly the Middle Ages), he probably had many resources and many opportunities to exploit those resources. It is likely that he knew and worked with the top medical people of his clan, along with the top clerics, philosophers, and even wizards of his time. Given his station, he was availed to the highest teachings about physics, chemistry, and the properties of life. The upshot here is that Dracula's high station in society, along with his crushing fall from that station, were critical precursors to the malevolent career that lay before him. Put another way, with these conditions about him, Dracula engaged every means at his disposal to ensure his perpetuity. Like Victor Frankenstein and so many of monster lore, he marshaled every elevated thought, every masterful trick, and every scientific oddity to erect the force, menace, and demon that he became. He proved the old adage that "hell hath no fury like a *narcissist* scorned," apart from and beyond its more tradi-tional association.

Yet for all his sense of discovery—all his transformative prow-ess—there was little satisfying about Dracula's course; even his aspirations to attain ever-lasting life (as one of the "undead") failed. Like the monsters before and after him, he sowed the seeds of his own destruction, not to mention that of countless others! Hence, the overriding question: How is it that multi-talented, multi-privileged savants like Frankenstein and Dracula turn monstrous? And conversely, how is it that others undergoing Frankenstein and Dracula's ordeals rise above and constructively transform their circumstances? One of the chief differences is social isolation. Both Frankenstein and Dracula labored alone; they lacked witnesses to mirror and support them. As previ-ously suggested, to be alone with trauma, to be cut off, and to have only oneself upon whom to rely, can and often does lead to very limited healing. The result is a floundering in one's own subconscious depths, a flailing with neither guide nor compass to orient one. And while a maturing process can occur in such circumstances, more often than not the core wound—the void or terror or mayhem—receives only a half-measure of support. Yet the core wound remains with all its attendant dynamics: defense and overcompensation, reactivity and fanaticism, blindness and monstrosity.

In sum, the monster tale throws open the whole range of possible responses to human tragedy. In *Dracula* it unveils the rot, corruption, and wickedness of a tormented soul; but it also elucidates the inventiveness of that soul, the wildly creative uses to which it can be put, and the potential for healing, illumination, and emotional bonding that inhere within it. The crux of constructive transformation, however, is presence, and without a witness to that presence—a guide or empathic peer—there is little support, let alone incentive, for this core undertaking. Dracula's problem, henceforth—like Frankenstein's before him—was psychical blind-ness: blindness to the battle required for psychospiritual restora-tion; blindness to the comfort, love, and sustainment required to surmount that battle; and blindness to the full and transformative possibilities that could ensue from that battle. All of these could only lead to his sad lot of drivenness, vitriol, and alienation.

An alternative to the wholly tragic outcomes of Dracula and Frankenstein is provided by *Eyes Without a Face,* a little known French classic that debuted in the cinema in 1959. In this mesmerizing yarn, a prominent plastic surgeon is faced with the most mortifying assignment of his life: the restoration of his daughter's deranged face. Following an auto accident, Christina (the surgeon's daughter) acquires a cruel disfigurement: her face is virtually torn from her skull. The question the movie poses is how and whether the formerly beautiful face should be restored, and who or what will restore it? From its inception to its riveting climax, *Eyes* becomes an object lesson in appearance values, the despair that ensues from such values, and the greed, desperation, and mercilessness that issue from the despair.

We can hardly blame him at first, but it appears that the elder physician will do everything in his power to rehabilitate his treasured offspring. By turns, however, the aspiration unfolds as perverse. At first he applies his know-how to re-attaching her face, but that quickly fails. Then he tries transplanting the faces of fresh corpses onto his daughter, but this too rapidly degenerates. Finally, desperately, he surmises that only the freshest living tissue will take hold on his child's skull. Therefore, with the assistance of his matronly companion, he conspires to kidnap "appropriate" young candidates. At the appointed hour, he anesthetizes these young surrogates, kills them, and transfers their faces to his daughter. The grim work takes months, and for months Christina is obedient to her father. In her own desperation to be restored, she passively goes through the motions of his orchestration, and though continually devastated by the repeated failures of that work, quietly gives herself over to the ensuing operation. She is not, however, without ambivalence toward the ordeal, and this ambivalence swells. While at first she is ignorant of her father's merciless methods, she soon learns the truth about them and begins to protest. She also periodically flies into rages—as well as deep despair—over her condition, and the hideous mask she must wear between operations is a jarring reminder of her lot. Like other legendary monsters, she is utterly isolated in her Byzantine and foreboding environs. She is like the lost little birds who flutter about in her father's dreary cages, or the pleading dogs imprisoned in their experimental chambers. She, too, is trapped, cut off, estranged from herself and the world, and all because of her appearance. At the same time, she experiences a growing affinity with these lab animals and their brethren. In breathtaking scenes of both terror and beauty, the young woman is both appalled by and sympathetic with her tormented compatriots. In time, her connection with them grows and belies a depth and wisdom that far exceeds the narcissistic authority of the father and the single-mindedness of his labors.

It is not until the end that the key question is asked—why is this grizzled man in surgical scrubs authorizing murder to improve his daughter's appearance? While the question looms over the tale throughout, it only comes into focus in the final tormenting moments. These are highlighted by the imprisonment of one last innocent victim and the culmination of the daughter's guilt, rage, and self-awakening in the light of that outrage. In the closing scenes, she is at last able to vindicate herself and to repudiate the banality of her father's crimes. She conclusively recognizes their futility, and she can at last face the abomination perpetrated on her surrogate and, indeed, on humanity itself.

In one decisive stroke, with the baying of the dogs in the background, she assaults her father and his assistant, frees the condemned surrogate from the operating table, and dashes out into the blustery night. There, in the wilds of the forest-edge, amid the splendor of the stars, she stops for a moment to contemplate her lot. She removes her mask, straightens up, and like a beatified princess, glides into the forested depths.

There are many entrancing layers to this macabre yet touching tale. The trial of a blighted young beauty and her self-absorbed, if also deeply pained and pitying, father is just the beginning. At its core, this story reflects the shock of derangement in a controlled and privileged life. It dramatizes the lengths to which victims will go to compensate for this shock, and, in the end, it demonstrates the dignity and power of being, beyond any self-absorbed fancies, at the core of the human quest. At the heart of *Eyes* is the classic monster motif—trauma, overcompensation, wonderment and fanaticism, but it diverges from most of its kin by emphasizing the wonderment dimension. The basis for this distinction perhaps relates to the film's lead, Christina. By casting a woman as the monster, *Eyes* takes on a very different hue and trajectory than the typical fare. Christina seems more vulnerable and at the same time more damaged than the standard male monstrosity. By the same token, she also seems more compassionate, more thoughtful, and in the end, more resilient than the latter. Another way to look at this point is that she was less inclined to become fanatical and lose her humanity over her condition—in the chasm of despair, she maintained a versatility, equanimity, and hope. But there was another element that seemed to help; she found connection. Whereas Frankenstein's monster and his ilk for the most part isolated themselves and were isolated from others, Christina found an alliance, interestingly enough, in nature. Nature and the animal world (the lab dogs and pigeons in particular) provided a witness to Christina's travails, and she in turn attuned to them. Through nature (and nature's own suffering, acceptance), Christina at last found an "ally" within which she could be both held and heard. She found a helpful witness that both resonated with and reflected back to her the larger identity of who she was, and in the light of that accompaniment, she was able to overcome herself (or as Nietzsche might have put it—to overcome her split-off identity). Through nature, moreover, Christina was no longer a pariah, a "shut-in," and an experiment; she could now understand that there was more to her injured existence, universes more, than her father, the culture, and even her half-torn face had conveyed to her.

In the end, Christina learned that at the same time that she was singularly damaged, she was also singularly free. At the same time she was degraded and diminished, at many other levels she was also lifted, ennobled. Her face, in the face of nature—in the face of dogs, pigeons, and forests—was a welcome face, a face of the eternal. To free herself from the vanity of images, Christina discovered that she had to free herself from the trivial and mundane, and from those to whom the trivial and mundane became enshrined. The world Christina stepped into in the aftermath of her grim rebellion, on that cool blustery evening, cannot be fully grasped; what can be grasped is that it far outmatched the world from which she exited.

The tragedy of unrequited love—of lust and longing and illusion—is nowhere as acutely illustrated as in Alfred Hitchcock's 1958 cinematic masterwork *Vertigo.* In this entrancing picture, a disabled San Francisco police officer, Scottie (played by Jimmy Stewart), is thrust into a bedazzling world. The story opens with Scottie's ill-fated chase of a suspect across skyscraper rooftops. Another officer also participates in the chase. At one awkward precipice, the other officer stumbles over a gutter and, despite Scottie's attempts to rescue him, plunges to his death. Scottie, meanwhile, also stumbles, but instead of following his condemned colleague, he manages to grab an overhang and gazes into the chasm below.

The scene quickly switches and Scottie is safely ensconced in his girlfriend Midge's apartment. (Midge is played by Barbara Bel Geddes.) Presumably Scottie was rescued, but he is obviously agitated. His leg is in a cast, and he has acquired acrophobia (fear of heights), along with the vertigo or dizziness that accompanies that fear. Midge tries to be consoling but cannot grasp the gravity of Scottie's ordeal. He is frustrated and guilt-ridden.

In the following scenes, an ex-college chum, named Gavin Elster, asks Scottie to investigate the strange behavior of his wife Madeline. Allegedly, she is obsessed with a deceased woman (who Elster later claims is a long-lost relative of Madeline's), and because she visits graves and speaks about morbid things, Elster is afraid that Madeline will hurt herself or someone else if she is not deterred. Scottie (somewhat reluctantly) agrees to discover all he can about her and to report his findings back to Elster.

Madeline (played by Kim Novak) is an ethereal beauty, and Scottie soon falls under her spell. She is an enigma though, and she leads him into bewildering situations. He follows her, for example, to the Palace of Fine Arts, where she stares at a painting of a deceased Spanish noblewoman. She stays at a hotel where this woman, Carlotta, allegedly lived. Finally, Madeline visits her gravesite. In time, Scottie perceives that Elster's concerns are valid. Madeline is indeed obsessed with Carlotta, a nineteenth century ancestor of her family (or so he believes). Scottie then makes an eerier observation: Carlotta committed suicide, and Madeline seems bent on emulating her! The first time she tries to take her own life by jumping into the San Francisco Bay. Scottie rescues her. The second time, however, is a different story. Here, Scottie must follow her up the winding staircase of the bell tower at San Juan Bautista Mission, near Monterey, California. Ascending the staircase, however, Scottie experiences vertigo and is unable to stop her. The next thing we hear is a scream, and what looks like Madeline's body crashes to the roof below.

Scottie is devastated by Madeline's apparent suicide and begins a long descent into depression. A hearing is conducted in which he is roundly condemned for negligence. He ends up in a sanitarium for a period, but he is beyond help, at least beyond that which can be offered by psychiatrists and his girlfriend, Midge.

Beleaguered and lovelorn, Scottie takes to the streets and discovers Judy, a rather plainly dressed working-class woman who has one outstanding trait—an uncanny resemblance to Madeline! The story's big twist occurs when Scottie discovers that Judy was indeed Madeline. She impersonated her so that Gavin Elster, who paid her for this role, could kill his wife at the bell tower. Elster, in other words, set Scottie up. He knew he had vertigo and that he would not be able to follow Madeline (who was really Judy) to the top of the bell tower. At that point, therefore, he pushed the body of his actual wife, Madeline, whom he had lured there and killed, out the bell tower and sent Judy back into obscurity.

Overtaken with rage at being duped, Scottie now forces Judy back to the scene of the crime—the bell tower. This time he is not curtailed by his vertigo and takes her to the very top. Judy pleads with him not to harm her and also to believe another complication, that she is in fact in love with him. While he contemplates this dilemma a nun suddenly appears and startles Judy into falling out of the tower to her death. Scottie is dumbstruck.

Now this film is obviously a goldmine of interpretation. It is a detective story, a love story, and a tale of innocence and revenge. However, at its deepest levels, *Vertigo* is a spell-binding study of awe—the thrill and anxiety of living, as well as the arrogance and humiliation of living. *Vertigo* begins with the humiliation of living. Humiliation is anatomized by Scottie's near fall and resultant trauma, his confinement to an injury, and his agonizing vertigo. At the start of the film Scottie is a broken man, with a withered sense of life. His girlfriend, Midge, is a comfort to Scottie, but she, too, is confined (in this case, by her conventionality) and unable to assist him out of his torment. *Vertigo* shows us that the first tragedy of humiliation can well be continued humiliation, continued diminution of powers and persistent debasement. It also shows us that the culture we encounter from this condition is not much of a benefit to us. It can soothe and placate, but does little to engage us and open us to our predicament.

Vertigo's second tragedy is Scottie's reactivity—the fanaticism that builds toward Madeline. In the absence of genuine healing, Scottie's desperation for emancipation, salvation, and wholeness become unbearable. Against this anguish, he seeks and envisions Madeline, the very embodiment of the paradisiacal. But the tragedy only intensifies, as the real Madeline is revealed to be a corpse, and Judy, the Madeline pretender, is exposed as a fraud.

Despite these calamities, however, *Vertigo* hints at yet a further psychospiritual horizon—the implication of redemption in both Scottie and Judy. This implication is subtle—it is not spelled out in headlines, but it is strongly suggested by gestures, images, and sentiments. It is betrayed, for example, by Scottie's double-take—revulsion yet fascination—at the edge of the precipice. It is evident when he chides Midge for her "motherliness," and when he boldly ascends a step-ladder to conquer his vertigo. It is intimated by his courageous and vulnerable moments with Judy. There are real signs of life in these poignant episodes and portents of break-throughs. Even at the fatal, final moment, when Judy declares her genuine love for Scottie, there is a glimpse of exhilarating transformation, a flicker of untrammeled promise.

Vertigo illustrates that genuine encounter, genuine restoration, is a persistent option in tragic circumstances; the question is, who or what will awaken people to this option, who or what will alert them to the openings betokened by their wounds? In Scottie's case, there clearly was no overt awakener to his potentials, no empathic witness. Still, given the innuendo of the film, one can imagine that Scottie *might* have chosen an alternative path. For example, instead of chasing a mirage, he could have meditated more over his circumstances, sorted through their various shadings, and consolidated them in practical, attainable actions. Had he done so, suggests the film, he would have averted the splitting that tore his life asunder: the perception of all-or-nothing impotency in the aftermath of his crisis, and the desperation, urgency, and relentlessness of his ill-fated quest. Correspondingly, he may have found vivacity in any of a number of personal realizations, through the creativity of an avocation during his recovery perhaps, or the radiance of the sun on a warm spring day, or possibly, just possibly, through a revitalized encounter with Midge, or the Madeline in a revitalized Judy.

Tragic Optimism and the Poignancy of Real Life

As suggested earlier, there are formidable benefits to a transformative view of tragedy. Like the hypothesized case of Toby, classic literature apprises us of some of these benefits—the potential for liberation, for example, in a deranged or excessive circumstance—but what are the real life implications of this view? What do real people report who have not only faced, but found meaning in their own life-trials—deaths, molestations, illnesses—and what do such people contribute to the world?

One of the first things we learn from such people is that they become what Frankl has termed "tragic optimists."[17] In other words, they develop a paradoxical sense of life, a sense of life that both includes and yet transforms the suffering they have undergone and that intensifies their day-to-day living. Tragic optimists become more sensitized to life, more present to their pain, and with equal fervor, more present to their joys. For tragic optimists, pain and joy fructify each other; frailty highlights life's preciousness, and vice versa. While pain is palpable to tragic optimists, it is not, in general, overriding; it is another side, facet, or opening—a strand in creation's fathomless mosaic.

Tragic optimists, those fluidly centered, are significantly less depressed, fearful, or dependent than many people, and, conversely, they are considerably more engaged, absorbed, and exploratory. They tend to be passionate, but not necessarily fixated. Their passion is more in processes, efforts, and hopes and less in polished truths.

Consider the plights of Sam and Andy who, along with eight of their cohorts, participated in what I believe will be a landmark study. This study, *The Experience of Tragic Optimism* by S.A. Rubin is noteworthy on several counts: it was conducted with self-described "tragic optimists"; it was convened at a locale of participants' choosing; it was collaborative; and it was in-depth.[18]

Sam, in his mid-40s, is a doctoral candidate in clinical psychology. Prior to his graduate education, he worked for 10 years at the "highest levels" of corporate business (p. 105).

Several years ago, Sam experienced three simultaneous blows: his father's death, the loss of a deep, long-term relationship, and a job transition. "So boom," Sam reports,

> pretty much everything died. My relationship with my girlfriend died, my relationship with my work died, and my relationship with my dad died. There was a keen awareness that I was the next one in line. I was, in the sense of here's my potential life staring me in the face… Every day of my life was without meaning and purpose. I was real busy at doing things that didn't mean anything (p. 125).

But, Sam elaborates:

The pain and suffering of death and loss opened up, on the other side, the optimistic part.... People don't all like me. Everybody doesn't want to stay with me. Every job isn't the great job. My dad is dead and I will be too. My experience of tragic optimism, it's the paradox. It is the awful and very freeing parts of my life—my grief [at dad's] death and this sense that I'm free. They don't seem to go together although I experience them simultaneously (p. 125).

"You can't have hope," Sam concludes,

unless you suffer the tragic, in my opinion. Because if everything's wonderful, it wouldn't even occur to you that it couldn't be. You have to experience dark—whatever dark is. You've got to be in the shadow to hope for light. Faith and possibility are very closely tied...for me (pp. 131–132).

Andy is a professor of clinical psychology and serves in several administrative capacities at a humanistic graduate school. He is married and has three children.

Andy's introduction to tragic optimism began with the "body blow" of his mother's death (p. 132). "There was this feeling," he observes,

this acute, poignant awareness of the loss; a sharp, gut-wrenching pain. That awareness is with me throughout this experience. Everything has a coloring, a shadow, a flavor of sadness, of hurt, of loss, of pain that feels like a broad scope of loss, that things aren't going to be the same again. That's also there the whole time (p. 133).

But then something different emerges in Andy's awareness. It is a sense of something larger and more restorative. Recalling his ride with his brother to their mother's funeral, he states:

It seemed so weird, like here we are driving to our mother's funeral. It was like so surreal. It's like you're walking a movie. And I'm noticing then, "I don't feel horrible. I'm not feeling horrible." And…I don't think everybody felt like that. Like my sister…went hysterical when my dad was giving away some of my mom's clothes…. But there was full presence. I didn't want to be anywhere else. Driving in that car and I'm just fully driving in this car with my brother. Everything's OK. I'm just [feeling], we're here. I love this person I'm with. This is just the guy I want to be—this is the sibling I would pick to be driving with, and there's a rightness about it. There's a feeling of attunement with the cosmic order (p. 108).

There was a sense to me of how beautiful it is and how lucky I was to have…my mother and all those incredible times we had. In many ways, this was the "worst thing that ever happened to me." In another way, it was one of the richest, fullest experiences I've ever had—this feeling of camaraderie with life (p. 166).

Sam and Andy are representative of a pioneering breed in my view. They are stable, loving, and even joyful people, in spite of life's anguish. They are whole, intact, and celebratory people, and they are also very grounded, humble, and grateful people. In contrast to so many today, they are broken people who not only live with, but draw upon and transform their brokenness. They are alive and vibrant people who do not require artifice, tricks, or distractions for their sustainment. What they do require, on the other hand, is raw openness, perspicacity, and awe.

In summary, S.A. Rubin elaborates:

The most significant discovery of my study…is the constellation of themes that I have organized within the framework of "existential spirituality." These constituents expressed by the co-researchers (participants) include: (1) rigorous philosophical inquiry into the nature of one's being-in-the-world; (2) faith in oneself (e.g., faith not externalized); (3) a self-transcendent stance: a sense of mission and full investment with something beyond oneself (e.g., one's lifework,…commitment to others—family, children); (4) living and engaging existential questions of meaning; (5) the capacity for…negotiating paradox; and (6) the experience of awe and existence as sacred ground as one identifies with the mystery and wonder of human existence.[19]

7

Struggle: The Forgotten Teacher

> The real struggle is with the *duende*....[T]he *duende* likes the edge of things, the wound, and...is drawn to where forms fuse themselves in a longing greater than their visible expressions.
>
> —Federico Garcia Lorca (in J.L. Gili, ed., *Lorca*, New York: Penguin, 1960, pp. 129, 136)

As suggested by the study on tragic optimism, the shift from a competency-based to an awe-based world will require more than literary allusions and institutional reformations—as critical as these will be. It will also require attunement. Attunement will be the base—the crux—upon which all subsequent reflection, discussion, and theorizing will revolve. Attunement is not simply intellectual appraisal or behavioral awareness, but (as the great poet above implies) it is a sustained encounter with the most intimate regions of experience. Among the forms that such attunement would take would be Who am I? What really matters? and How can I *live* what really matters? In the section to follow, we will consider one of the signal modalities for attunement—depth therapy. Specifically, we will look at the strengths of that modality, the threats that beset it, and the potential it holds for a revitalized ethos.

Depth Therapy as Social Vision

They say it's passé. They say it's a luxury that most cannot afford. And yet depth therapy, the object of these epithets, is arguably the most radical social development since the advent of the Enlightenment. Further, depth therapy is both a byproduct of and reaction against that very movement. The tale of depth therapy is a long and complex one (see Ellenberger's *Discovery of the unconscious* for a start).[1] Both Enlightenment rationalism and Romantic transcendentalism are its forebears. A poignant blend of art and science, spiritual openness and scientific discernment, depth therapy offers—even today—an abundance of liberating respites, a healing ground, with few contemporary equivalents.

At the same time though, there are legitimate critiques of this rarified and laborious activity. For example, depth therapy *is* preponderantly upper class; it *can* be self-indulgent; and it *does* degenerate into intellectual "wheel-spinning." That said, however, none of these problems are insurmountable, and some (e.g., the self-indulgence and intellectual wheel-spinning) have already begun to be remedied.[2] As a depth practitioner of over twenty years, having partaken in the lives and journeys of many, I am convinced of the viability of depth therapy—and not just as a form of individual healing, but as a form of collective enlivening. The vehemence of my feeling cannot be overstated—depth therapy at its best is the most hopeful, the most revitalizing, and the most emancipating of contemporary social visions.

Experience is the basis for my conclusion. Depth therapy at its best values the whole human being and the richest possible ranges of human experience within the most suitable parameters of support. It recognizes the needs for exploration, adventure, and play within the human social arena, but also, and with equal fervor, the importance of safety, structure, and sustenance. In short, depth therapy illuminates a form or pattern by which awe and the fluid center *can be lived out*. We have already explored some of these implications with awe-based work and educational settings. Now it is time to view the larger picture, to place awe, the fluid center, and carnival at center stage in our contemporary lives. To do this, we need the metaphor and the practical, palpable exemplar of depth therapy.

Depth Therapy and Why it is so Needed Today

Depth therapy is the theory and practice of depth understanding; it is the theory and practice of healing or restoring the whole human being, from the subconscious to the conscious and from the physiological to the psychospiritual. Depth therapy addresses not only symptoms of dis-ease (e.g., sleeplessness, weight gain), but the experiences—attitudes and sensibilities—that underlie and inform those symptoms. Depth therapy is holistic, but it is also realistic; it acknowledges our daunting thresholds, impotencies, and fragilities, along with our breathtaking possibilities. It is depth therapy's refusal to shortchange life-experience—its integrity—that is so needed today. Depth therapy teaches its participants to square off with themselves, to get "down and dirty," and to *contend* with their conflicting lives. There is too little contending today. Too many are gliding through or stumbling past or simply missing their lives. As a result there is a derangement: denial and displacement have become the norms, whereas passion and struggle have become deviations. Society is set to bypass human pathos and angst. Are the tranquilized results what we prefer? Let us pause—deeply.

I have the greatest admiration for my clients and others who take the immensely challenging step to face, take stock of, and potentially transform their lives. In essence, these clients are doing what ought to come naturally in a more life-affirming, awe-illuminating milieu. The problem is that most of us are not afforded such a milieu, and concerted self-exploration must be relegated to surrogates, such as consulting rooms. And what do we witness in such rooms?

Consider Mary, the 240-pound woman who wrote furiously in her journal about her fear of visibility.[3] Seduced and teased as a child, Mary had negligible trust in men, little trust in herself in the presence of men, and minute trust in the culture that tacitly assented to these calamities. Yet here she was, at 30-years-old, declaring her commitment to re-envision and re-assemble her life. Here she was spending hours of the evening dashing off reams of pages about the pain, injustice, and outrages of her life, but also at the same time the dreams, desires, and possibilities that could be her life. She would read from and share reflections about her entries, and she would scrap tirelessly with them. Back and forth, she would shift; between searing self-abasement and rising self-attunement, between depleting worry and replenishing confidence. Her struggle displayed all the earmarks of the depth excursion, the depth entanglement, that precedes restoration. She, like many therapy clients, had to straddle between contending life-paths, to sift out the intimations of those life-paths, and to consolidate a plan, direction, and vision that was based on those intimations. Following months of such wrangling and deep preverbal explorations, she gradually and doggedly re-emerged. She found that capitulating to her father, the culture, and the taboo of asserting herself was no longer tolerable and that changes had to occur.

Her first step, which I encouraged, was to allow herself to be angry enough, indignant enough, to halt her automatic binging, and to peer into the void it replaced. Instead of instantly seeking food as a refuge, therefore, she instituted a pause in her experience; she allowed the fears and hurts to percolate. Yet in this percolation was much more than fears and hurts. She realized, for example, that she no longer had to be so readily panicked over being seen by others, that she would not inexorably be attacked by the person she feared, and that, greatest of all, she had a value and truth that she could not squander. Regardless of her obesity, she realized, *she* had worth, a tender, loving essence inside her, yearning to be felt, heard, and held.

Her second step was the long and arduous process of losing her excess girth and of confronting the barriers to this toilsome process. It's not that she felt an obligation to lose pounds or even that this ordeal was mandatory for her physical health. All of these "supposed tos" were increasingly peripheral to her. By contrast, that which was mandatory for her was an internal rightness about losing her weight. She did not want to go into a program until she felt clear that health, attractiveness, and integrity were necessary for *her*—not for some imagined other.

Following this clarification, she embarked on an eight month trial with a powder diet as a replacement for meals. This course had its own thorny challenges, but she met them well. On the one hand, the powder was "easy," because it was readily available, habit-forming, and required little forethought. On the other hand, precisely because it was *not* food, the powder presented Mary with opportunities to reassess her associations to food. Among these associations was the comfort value of food, the special linkages to sweets, and the pleasure of cooking. Chief among Mary's discoveries was that behind all these compelling features of food was the daunting capacity of food to protect. From the standpoint of protection, Mary realized, food was not simply a distraction or a pleasurable obsession; it was a refuge from perceived oblivion. By eating the powder, and, particularly, by attending to the feelings, sensations, and images conjured up by her consumption of the powder, Mary learned to confront death, the "death" (or brutality) she associated with her nakedness, beauty, and rawness when removed from her culinary refuge. As a result, she began to cope better with that death anxiety. She became less anxious and acquired new patterns of self-support—such as speaking up for herself and associating with caring company. She also found freedom in her newfound visibility, particularly the freedom to play. She indulged in play like a kid on her first visit to a beach. She ran and worked out and hiked, and simply reveled in her newfound, 130-pound mobility. She also reveled in her newfound attractiveness to men.

But, as with so many who embark on the dieting path, Mary eventually relapsed. After eight invigorating months, Mary discovered another layer to her agonizing ordeal: She had yet to confront her rage. Mary and I spent many subsequent months addressing this rage and the symptoms, fears, and difficulties that accompanied it. Although much of this rage centered on her father, some of it was directed at herself, the world, and me, as a representative of that world. Eventually, after three arduous years, Mary was able to align with a new part of herself, a part that could acknowledge but also transcend debilitating wounds. She found her way back to sports, for example, and a regenerated career, but, most importantly, she rediscovered life.

Like another weight loss survivor, "Karen," Mary rediscovered life's vibrancy in all its glorious complexity.

Here is what Karen had to say after her own three-year journey:

> I wish I could tell you that being a size twelve is all wonderful but I'm finding out that being awake and alive is a package deal. I don't get to go through the line and pick only goodies. On one side is wonder, awe, excitement and laughter—and on the other side is tears, disappointment, aching sadness. Wholeness is coming to me by being willing to explore ALL the feelings.
>
> So....275 pounds later, my life is a mixture of pain and bliss. It hurts a lot these days but its real. It's my life being lived by me and not vicariously through a soap opera....I don't know where it's all heading, but one thing I know for sure, I'm definitely going.[4]

What if more of us could "go" where Karen and Mary are headed? What if more of us had depth therapy as an alternative? These are core contemporary problems—core challenges—and in the next section we shall explore why.

Transhumanism and The Transhumanist Threat

Gradually, and with increasing ferocity, human identity is being "chipped" away—literally as well as figuratively. There are four ominous (although potentially wondrous) technological innovations that are about to rock our world—nanotechnology (the miniaturization of mechanical devices), robotics (the mechanical imitation of human functioning), genetic engineering (the manipulation of genetic DNA), and designer drugs (the targeting and medicating of negative moods).

Notwithstanding the marvels of these innovations, enormous questions are looming about their influence. Chief among these is what will they portend for human identity? Who (or what) will the human being become, if he or she is tethered by microchips or instant changes in personality? Who or what will become of human greatness—desire, aspiration—if human vulnerability is assuaged? How is a mechanically assisted brain or a synthesized musculature experienced? Can touch be programmed? What of sensuality, reverie, and imagination? People, not gods, will have to decide.

Perhaps human beings are destined to become cyborgs, hybrids of robotic flesh. A growing movement appears to countenance this direction. They call themselves "transhumanists," and they urge global psychophysiological change.[5] Transhumanists call for a "post-human" world, a world in which disease is all but eradicated, body parts are instantly replacable, minds are immediately alterable, and thoughts can be synthetically controlled. In theory, transhumanists believe, human consciousness will "download" the entire human knowledge-base, and in this "utopia," no discipline, no programable information byte, will be spared.

Yet, it is not so much the transhumanist proclamations that are at issue. They are clearly overdrawn in some areas and pertain only marginally to our immediate, inchoate circumstances. That which is at stake, however, is the logic of the transhumanists' proclamations. They are touching a pulse which many dare not consider, let alone perceive. It is not the prospect of cyborg invasion that should trouble us; it is the prospect of losing ourselves in that invasion, of forfeiting our interpersonal ethics, and of forgetting our aliveness in the face of it that are the real dangers. While it may be worth the cost in given circumstances, there is one point on which many would concur: artificiality dulls. It dulls our relationship to ourselves, our relationship with others, and our awareness of our bodies. A pill can (and perhaps should) help us get through the night, but it is not, in my view, an enduring "solution." Physically healthy babies are emphatically desirable, but uniform, invulnerable babies are a travesty of mortal life. Artificial organs can be a blessing, but menacing trade-offs should ever be apprised. For example, the provision of artificial body parts, and particularly those affecting mental and emotional acuity, should be made with profound forethought, intensive deliberation, and keen attunement as to their personal and interpersonal effects.

While the revolution in human biotechnology is a reality, our response to it is far from foreordained. Myriad inquiries must be put to this accelerating specter, and the question of struggle must be chief among them. Struggle is the catalyst to profound appraisal of one's condition. It is the searchlight that vivifies the rivaling and fractious sides of ourselves and the diverse facets of our possibility. From my own experience as a therapist, it is precisely these vivifications that lead to our fuller, more orchestrated illumination—about who we are, what essentially matters to us, and where we are, or are willing to be headed. The vivifications, moreover, are the seedbed of what Rollo May termed intentionality—the whole-bodied, impassioned involvement in a value or direction and the whole-bodied, impassioned transformation of a life.[6] Consider some of the plights of my clients: If Mary (discussed earlier) did not grapple with her terror of vulnerability, she would not have overcome her obesity; if John, another client, did not face his reckless grandiosity, he would not have nurtured intimacy; if Ted did not encounter his career inertia, he would not have found his impassioned landscape photography. And the stories go on. But what is abundantly clear to me, as with many who preside at such crucibles, is that the replacement of struggle is too often the eradication of a hard-won resiliency, a hard-fought fulfillment in life. Fulfillment does not come through eradication, it does not come through replacements—it is not *appreciated* through replacements—it must come, on the other hand, through a profound sense of awareness, a profound sense of choice, and a profound commitment. These we cannot mechanize, and we should not delude ourselves that we can.

PART III:

The Fluid Center of Faith

8

Between Anarchy and Dogma: Toward a Faith in the Inscrutable[1]

[T]he most important thing...to know [is] that beyond the absurdity of one's own life, beyond the human viewpoint,...there is the fact of the tremendous creative energies of the cosmos that are using us for some purposes we don't know.

—Ernest Becker ("The heroics of everyday life: A theorist of death confronts his own end," *Psychology Today,* April, 1974, p. 78)

Let's face it: With regard to faith and ethics today, we're between a rock and a hard place. The rock is extremist-fundamentalist religion and the hard place is postmodern free-market anarchy. Just consider the battles now raging, from back alleys in the Middle East to boardrooms on the East Coast.

The fluid center, on the other hand, provides an alternative to these debilitating extremes: it implies conviction, but also questioning; humility, but also wonder. What, then, are the roles of faith and ethics in such an outlook?

Let me propose the following:

Behind every bounded faith resides an evolving, indefinite faith. Beyond every bounded god resides an expanding, indecipherable god. Tillich calls this god the "God beyond God" or the marvel and mystery of creation.[2]

The marvel and mystery of creation are beyond every "truth," belief, and measure; they are beyond every beyond.

Behind every monocular view is a transcendent question, "but what is beyond that?" Whenever we are spiritually "caught"—whenever we specify, identify, or classify—we are caught short. The inscrutable cannot be specified; it must be lived with, reveled in, and suffered from. Captivating as they may be, gods and goddesses, idols and icons, obsessions and fixations are but pale stand-ins—substitutes and buffers—for the inscrutable. Even the Absolute or the Atman or the Void—to the degree they are decipherable—are but veneers.

To be sure, veneers may be all we have; they evoke the sublime, suggests Burke[3]; they are the vehicles, carriers, fragments of the divine, echoes Tillich.[4] "Something is holy to everyone," Tillich expounds, "even to those who deny the holy."[5] But what is key for these thinkers is that pieces of the holy must not be confused with the holy itself—which is the inscrutable. Whereas definable gods (such as those in the Old and New Testaments, ancient myth, and popular culture) polarize us—either containing and belittling us on the one hand, or inflating and exaggerating us on the other—the inscrutable fosters neither. That which the inscrutable does foster, by contrast, is wholeness—not puritan or absolute wholeness, but dynamic, paradoxical wholeness. The inscrutable evokes our humility and our possibility at the same time, but instead of dictating these conditions from on high, it inspires *us* to negotiate them, to find our way *within* them. The result of this understanding is that devotees of the inscrutable are more inclined to see *through* their investments and are less driven by them. They are less entrapped—either by false hope or false despair—and they are enlivened by a poignancy to life, an overview, that heightens each attendant moment.

The way to the inscrutable is through struggle. Struggle jolts the system, dents the armor, and jars the rails. But struggle is only the beginning. The shock and the awakening are only preparatory. The next crucial question is how and whether one pursues, engages with, and emerges from one's struggle. To the degree one does, one can see beyond it; one can both acknowledge, identify with, and yet somehow be more than that with which one contends.

Expediency, the catchword of our time, is not a route to the inscrutable. It is a route to the definable, the consolable, and the delimiting. One cannot through gimmickry partake of the fruits of vibrancy or of the profound and emancipating. There are no tricks to cultivating awe. The danger today is that we delude ourselves into believing in such tricks, that we mistake Isaiah Berlin's jigsaw puzzle universe for the brute and throbbing one into which we are thrust.[6] As suggested previously, almost every cutting-edge technology poses this danger; virtually every designer drug, genetic manipulation, and robotic innovation holds the potential for abominable self-delusion. While we can be aided, and, indeed, miraculously transformed by these developments, we must not lose touch with their partiality and their envelopment by the inscrutable.

Ethically, one of the greatest dangers of the new technology is jadedness. The more we become jaded, the less we acknowledge Mystery. The less we acknowledge Mystery, the more we lose touch with its current. The current of Mystery, of the inscrutable, is amazement. Whatever one wants to label this amazement—God, Love, Brahman, Nirvana, Prana, Buddha, Jesus, Creatrix, or even Randomization, Process, or Energy—it's simply too incredible to sweep aside, downplay, or tout as nondivine. This divinity has enormous implications, even as an inscrutable divinity, perhaps *especially* as an inscrutable divinity. Let us look at some of those here.

One doesn't need a directive and definable god to feel the presence of divinity. If we begin with the inscrutable, we begin with a sense of something incomprehensible at work. We begin with awe. This sense infuses everything that we do, feel, and think, and it affects all our relations with the world. If creation is amazing and incomprehensible, then everything that partakes in creation must be seen as equally amazing and incomprehensible. It follows, moreover, that everything must be treated, to the extent possible, as amazing and incomprehensible.

Just where does this axiom lead? It leads to the foundational religious concepts of respecting the stranger, caring about the neighbor, and so on. Yet it goes beyond the reflexive obedience to commands. It embraces the obedience which cannot, in the end, be declined, the command which cannot, in total, be shunned, the command of creation itself. This is the command of the inscrutable, the majestic beyond, which at one point or another we must heed.

The key here is that the respect commanded by the inscrutable is not at all of the neatly codified variety, such as that found in religious tracts. It is of a wholly different nature. In contrast to religious tracts, the inscrutable compels a mutable respect, a respect that leans on humanity. This respect, it seems to me, is the optimal arbiter for our ambiguous condition. Just as one can't apply a "fits all" product to a diverse and opinionated populace, one can't force a "fits all" ethic to a complex and changing existence. This ethics of ambiguity, as de Beauvoir termed it,[7] is not at all whimsical or arbitrary; it is not "anything goes" behavior. It is an ethic that calls upon the deepest energies of democracy, the fullest engagements of dialogue, and the keenest perceptions of context. This kind of ethics is not simply "situational" ethics, as that approach is conventionally understood. By contrast, the ethics I propose is an "awe-based" situational ethics; it is an ethics infused by the thrill and anxiety of living and the reverence, humility, and wonder of living. While other situational ethics tend to resort to intellectual or consensus-based criteria, an awe-based ethics is ever attuned to the whole, the embodied, and the relational in its deliberations (see for example, Carol Gilligan's inspired critique of the cognitive-developmental moral approach of Lawrence Kohlberg).[8] In short, an awe-based ethics is attuned to the many levels of our relationship to the problem in question, to the inscrutable as a whole, which of necessity incorporates the heart, head, and body.

This holistic view is precisely what contemporary forms of pluralistic decision-making lack and therefore suffer from in their rivalries with other ethical forms. The problem is that many of the other ethical forms, e.g., fundamentalism and sectarianism of all kinds, despite any counterbalance they offer, fall woefully short of holism themselves. Consider, for example, the Taliban of Afghanistan, who rave against "godless" capitalism, but treat women as inferiors, forbid secular education, and ban expressions of emotion.

Yet by beginning with awe and the inscrutable, there is no instant path. The path, in fact, becomes an article of faith, a leap. At some point one has to leap. The question is from whom or what does that leap emerge—a religious decree, a parental command, a governmental law? Or is there a more personal derivation?

Through struggle, intentional living, and openness, one can find awe-based faith. But this faith is very different than the reflexive faith of disciples, the expedient faith of marketers, or the obsessive faith of fanatics. This is a faith wrought from the *encounter* with these singular faiths. It is a faith wrought from the encounter with the myopic, the fleeting, and the one-dimensional—a faith wrought from pain but not confined by pain. It is a faith born of deep self-inquiry, deep presence to the results of that inquiry, and deep trust in the unfolding of the results. It is a faith born of confidence that one can survive one's intense grappling, but it is not just a faith in survival; it is a faith in that which permits survival to occur.

Awe-based faith entails a "giving up when there's nothing left," as Ernest Becker put it, a placing of one's trust in the "tremendous creative energies of the cosmos" to work through and with us when we are spent.[9] The key here, however, is "when we are spent." Too many circumvent this arduous faith and seek the easy, though life-draining, course.

Enough of theory though—what might an awe-based ethics, an ethics of the inscrutable, look like in practice?

Sub Specie Aeternae and the Capacity to be Moved

An awe-based ethics begins with the capacity to be moved.

The capacity to be moved is one of the least appreciated pillars of child development. By the capacity to be moved I do not mean mere sentimentality. This is a partialization (polarization) of the capacity to be moved. What I do mean, on the other hand, is the maximal capacity to be impacted by experiences—to pause and to feel and to ponder. Secondly, it is the maximal capacity to be impacted by the entire range of human experience, and not merely those aspects which are dramatic or ready-at-hand. Too often we fall victim to those debilitating aspects and forget our subtler natures.

The capacity to be moved, to pause, and to be present is as integral to child-raising as the capacity to speak, teach, and discipline. While children's capacity to be moved is to some extent natural, it is the parents' task, as I view it, to bolster that capacity. It is the parents' challenge, likewise, to allow themselves to be moved, to be profoundly affected, in the child's presence; and it is the child's challenge as he or she grows up to keep the capacity to be moved alive—whether at play, at school, or with friends. Awe-based faith and a faith in the inscrutable begins with the capacity to be moved. The capacity to be moved is the seedling, the spark, for a capacity for awe; and the capacity for awe is the catalyst for a faith in the inscrutable. Put another way, the capacity to be moved is the rudiment of an enlarged view: the view of exuberance, for example, above and beyond enjoyment; or of angst over and above fear; or of puzzlement over and above certitude. Each of the aforementioned exemplify the enlarged view.

When an alive, aware, and moved parent embraces a child, countless impulses are interchanged. The embrace becomes an event, an experience, that cannot help but impress itself far beyond the instant. In fact, it is my contention that a series of such embraces yield to a life-long body memory. This memory, the impression of a warm and loving body, a body that unconditionally accepts, revels in, and celebrates the subject of its embrace, provides a fathomless well of sustenance throughout adult life. This sustenance, furthermore, provides hope to people, trust in others, and faith in the universe. But it has an even weightier role—it is the cradle of the enlarged view I spoke of earlier, the enlarged vision. Without a sense of sustenance—a sense of inner support, confidence, or strength—it is very difficult to bear emotionality, and without emotionality, one's view is collapsed.

The capacity to be moved, therefore, solidifies through others' capacities to be moved, through others' support of such movement. These "others" include caretakers, parents, and institutions. Following from the capacity to be moved is the capacity to experience the largeness of life, the amazement, wonder, and multi-facetedness of life. While thoughts and behaviors can give us glimpses of this large-ness, they are, of necessity, fragmentary. Thoughts are fragmented by concepts, and behaviors are delimited by physical abilities. Feel-ings, on the other hand, have no such curtailments. Their nature is atmospheric—as Heidegger would suggest—and embraces indefi-nite perceptual horizons (see also Nussbaum, 2001).[10]

The capacity to be moved is commensurate with Spinoza's no-tion of "under the aspect of eternity"(or *"sub specie aeternae"*).[11] To live under the aspect of eternity (or the cosmic), according to Spinoza, heightens our day-to-day consciousness. It does this in two basic ways: by realizing the profound context within which consciousness resides, and by placing a priority on that profound context, a priority on the consciousness of infinity, which suffuses every instance of living. In contrast to the latter, as Spinoza elabo-rates, we often preoccupy ourselves with narrow or uninspiring horizons, debasing relationships, or idle pursuits.

The lesson here for caretakers is to provide the template for *sub specie aeternae,* to foster and encourage diverse childhood experiences, from sadness to gladness, unsettlement to bliss, repulsion to zeal. Through such facilitation (to the degree ap-propriate), children can learn to trust their internal groping, trust the relationships that participate in that groping, and, hopefully, eventually trust in the mystery to which all groping must submit. A distinction must be drawn here, however, between enabling and amplifying childhood experience. Too often today, childhood experience is amplified or encouraged to amplify. This amplifica-tion takes place through the media, where sensationalism reigns; through marketing, where hype predominates; and through edu-cation, where accelerated learning is glorified. Yet, amplification of children's capacity to feel is not the same as cultivation of their capacity to be moved. While the former is comparatively forced, the latter is comparatively self-discovered; and while the former is imposed from without, the latter is evoked from within. There is a vast difference between these two modalities, and their conse-quences are also vast. The child who is bombarded by amplifica-tion is impeded from illumination—from immersion, presence, and self-exploration. Conversely, he or she is hurtled into an emotional meteor shower, an electrification, within which no single thought or feeling can be concentrated upon, and all must be juggled at once. There seem to be few genuine spaces for freedom in such a world, few chances to discern; but that which does predominate is haste, flippancy, and insatiability. The insatiability, moreover, fuels a lessening tolerance for pauses, for delay, and for fructifying self-inquiry. Most of what one wants, one wants *now*, this *instant*, and there is a decreasing premium on the quality or substantiality of the desire. The main issue is the desire to be fed, gorged, sated—there is more of an emphasis on quantity than on quality and on stimulation over discrimination. The upshot is that rich emotional nuances are lost in such a cavalcade and the loud and accentuated are prized. In light of these trends, is it any wonder that life is such a blur to many youth today and that more nuanced activities, such as reading, personal and interpersonal reflection, and intellectual discovery are regarded with disdain? One middle-school principal, Emily Gaddis, put it this way: "[The kids] have grown up with technology, in an entertainment age of video games and all that flash. Compared to video games, school is slow, deliberate, routine. Kids get bored easily, and we struggle every day against that."[12] The article in which this principal's words appeared went on to illustrate a student's home environment, which supported her description: "He had a television at the base of his bed with a choice of video games, but the seventh grader could not produce a book he owned."[13]

Yet the fault for these excesses cannot be placed at the student's or the parents' doorstep alone—we must look at the institutions, both economic and political, that fuel the need for manic, technology-driven lifestyles. Further, we must look at the so-called remedies these institutions provide for the fallout from their own product lines, which tend to be as hyper and semiconscious as the problems themselves. This caveat is illustrated every day by numerous contemporary elixirs—pills, shopping, Internet surfing, channel hopping, and tabloid gazing. Then there are the more legitimated patch-up jobs—each of which has been associated with calamitous after-effects—such as twelve week anger management classes for self-hating teens, three-day "stabilization" programs for disturbed street-dwellers, monthly medication check-ins for embittered 50-year-olds, and life-long neuroleptics for latch-key kids.[14]

By the same token, I am not advocating emotional Puritanism here. Nor am I suggesting that feelings should not be temporarily or artificially intensified, or for that matter, relieved. There is, of course, a place for such undertakings, as anyone who has enjoyed a good rock concert or numbed himself or herself with an occasional intoxicant will attest. The question is how can we intensify or relieve feelings in the service of an overall deepening of those feelings, a deepening of the capacity to be moved? This is a far from simple problem, but if we are to avoid the desiccation of our culture, it is an essential one to face. We can start to face it by valuing struggle, reflection, and dialogue, precisely the dimensions which are disparaged in today's ethos. To the degree we, as caretakers, can be sensitized to our children's reactivity, the more we are in a position to support or challenge them when that reactivity crosses usual thresholds. What are these thresholds? Each caretaker, of course, must judge this problem individually, but to the extent that a given caretaker has the capacity to be moved him or herself, and has a faith in that capacity, then he or she will be in an improved position to respond to a child, and to respond responsibly. That means acting from within the context of a child's total situation. Such a situation includes his or her resources, needs, and anxieties—as well as quality of activity. It may be, therefore, that in some situations the caretaker would assent to a given amplification (e.g., a film), sensing that it may serve (or at least not impede) a child's evolving emotionality. Correspondingly, a caretaker might enable a child to rage, to fight, or to stew in a given circumstance, or, in still other contexts, he or she may hastily intervene. The chief questions are: How present is the caretaker to the child, how capable is the child of being present to and sorting through a situation him or herself, and how urgent is the given problem? The answers to each of these questions will depend on caretaker attunement to the widest range of a child's emotionality; and that attunement will set the stage for a direct, awe-informed, and trusting interpersonal bond.

From this sensitizing bond, from struggle and the willingness to work it through, the child can gain what Erickson terms basic trust.[15] The trust is basic in that it is dependent on one essential element—the relationship with the caretaker. Yet the trust, as Erickson also well knew, has greater implications, not just for the child in society, but, for the child—and later adult—before creation itself. Drawing on this basic trust in people, faith can develop in creation itself. Faith is contingent on this basic trust; it is contingent on the ability to feel anchored in oneself—one's body—and to feel secure enough to open to that which is unknown. Just as the child opens to the unknown parent through struggle, he or she is also challenged through struggle to open to the unknown of creation. But a child cannot engage in such an undertaking if he or she is estranged from feelings or from the risk of feelings. There can be no risk where there is no courage and there can be no courage where there is no struggle.

The faith in being is the most challenging form of trust. Indeed, such faith goes beyond trust because trust is relegated to the knowable realm. While the knowable realm may not be presently known, it can generally be accessed, inquired upon, or inspected. Faith, on the other hand, is an investment in an unknowable realm, the realm of the inscrutable. To have faith in the inscrutable is the most radical trust that one can attain. It is a trust in the tremendous forces of change, a wider order, despite our total blindness as to that order's origin, nature, or aims. To the degree that we can accept this puzzlement, allow the weight of it to sink in, we can live with a sense of eternity, an awe, that can ever carry us forth.

But again, we must begin with caretakers, the culture, and the milieu. We must begin with the development of trust—the inner knowing that no matter how many times one has faltered or disappointed, someone was there who helped one survive and carry on. We need to know there was a witness who cared. This development of trust leads to a sense of internal freedom—a freedom of both accessibility and expressiveness, as Bugental has put it.[16] Accessibility is characterized by the maximal capacity to experience life, to range within, whereas expressiveness is distinguished by the optimal capacity to draw out that range, "to let oneself be known."[17]

Within relative degrees, the internally free person can be understood as the internally integrated person. Since he or she has a sizable capacity to be moved, to access and express his or herself, he or she experiences fewer areas of taboo, fewer domains of constraint, and fewer impulses to inflate. In consequence, such a person's life is generally heightened, enriched, and enlarged.

Despite these great strengths, however, even the internally (relatively) free must buckle under at some points, flounder, and rely on greater powers. Even the hardiest among us must have faith, lest they wither. The question is what kind of faith, and how does it differ from that of the conventionally religious?

There are two chief differences between the faith of the internally (relatively) free and that of the conventionally religious. The first hinges on the role of inquiry; the second, on specificity. Whereas the conventionally religious tend to resist inquiry about their faith, the internally (relatively) free tend to question their faith consistently; and whereas the conventionally religious tend to experience their faith as clear and specific, the internally (relatively) free tend to experience theirs as enigmatic and evolving. To put it more concretely, the conventionally religious tend to invest in divinities that are near-at-hand, that give them firm directions, and that divide the world into comforting categories (such as good and bad, Christian and non-Christian, sinful and moral, and so on). The result of this purview is that, ostensibly at least, life becomes orderly, investments containable, and difficulties minimized. The internally (relatively) free, on the other hand, tend to invest in spirits/forces that lie far beyond conventional parameters, that yield minimal directions, and that apprehend the world in its diversity, complexity, and immensity. The result of their purview is that life becomes adventurous, investments daring, and difficulties animating.[18]

The freer the person, then, the more likely it is he or she will grapple with life's challenges—even if this grappling is quiet, contemplative, or communal. Conversely, the freer person is less likely to shortchange him or herself, give up prematurely, or settle for the easy fix. Such grappling, moreover, does not at all preclude religious types. Some of the most pious devotees, such as Mahatma Gandhi, Martin Luther King, Jr., and Thomas Merton, were among the most active inquirers. The question is to whom, or what, were they pious before? The answer generally was broad, deep, and enigmatic. The freer the individual, the less willing that person is to dwell on air-tight proclamations or theological roadmaps. Even in complete surrender, he or she must be free. This latter point is precisely why freer people invest in the remotest, most ambiguous gods (the Gods beyond Gods, as Tillich put it). By contrast, Gods who are clearer, more direct, or more accessible are more constraining for these people—and more dangerous, potentially, as history has amply demonstrated. Consider, for example, the specificity of the instruction booklet issued to the September 11, 2001 terrorists. Concerning the night before their hijacking, the booklet dictated: "You should pray, you should fast. You should ask God for guidance…. Purify your heart and clean it from all earthly matters. The time of fun and waste has gone. The time of judgment has arrived."[19]

Spiritual abandon, or the leap of faith, is of necessity ambiguous for the relatively free. He or she will not leap into the ready arms of a cult figure, biblical deity, or religious reverend. Nor, on the other hand, will he or she reflexively submit to any secular leader, institution, or icon. When he or she does "leap," it will be toward the farthest beyond, the least definable power, and the most daunting horizon. Even then the person will "reside" in ambiguity—albeit the most impressive kind!

The solace of amazement is the highest solace to which the free can aspire. While others experience solace in salvation, the free discover it in astonishment, mystery, and unfolding. While others perceive salvation in the solace of the literal or the local or the ready-at-hand, the free experience hope in the solace of the implicit, the vast, and the farthest reaching.

The Temptation to Partialize (A *Human* Predicament)

Finding faith in the inscrutable and solace in amazement is formidable. Even those who ostensibly support it very often stray
from it, stray from the capacity to be maximally moved. Carl
Jung, for example, labored for much of his professional life with
faith in the inscrutable. He advanced sweeping theories of spiritual regeneration, penetrating studies of mystical transformation,
and inspiring analyses of mythic emancipation; yet throughout
his lifetime he repeatedly flirted with partializing, rigidifying,
and deemphasizing the indefinite. He did this with his theories of
archetypes, his formulaic language, and his ethnocentrism. Consider the following passage, written in 1923, where he decries the
"mutilation" of "Germanic man":

> Like Wotan's oaks, the gods were felled and a wholly incon-
> gruous Christianity, born of monotheism on a much higher
> cultural level, was grafted on the stumps. The Germanic man
> is still suffering from this mutilation.... It therefore seems a
> grave error if we graft yet another foreign [e.g., semitic] growth
> onto our already mutilated condition. This craving for things
> foreign and faraway is a morbid sign.[20]

And in another place Jung writes: "The Aryan unconscious has a
higher potential than the Jewish; that is the advantage and disadvantage of a youthfulness not yet fully estranged from barbarism."[21]

I cite these passages neither to scapegoat Jung nor to impugn
the luminosity of his work—I draw from much of it myself. However, any one of us, even the most broad-minded, can lapse into
the fragmentary. The road to a generous and awe-encompassing
faith is a truly elusive one. Many have embarked on it only to
stumble on blind spots—the easy, the comforting, or the momen-
tary. There is always the temptation to idealize, as Hazel Barnes
suggests in her groundbreaking ethical commentary.[22] The task
of the leader, philosopher, or thinker is to respond to rather than
react rashly before such tendencies. But such response-ability, is

not merely an intellectual byproduct; it is a byproduct of one's entire orientation to the world, one's entire bodily awareness. To be maximally free, moreover, one must respond with one's entire being, with maximal access to one's being. Monocular focus on one's ethnic heritage, no matter how transiently justified, does not preserve one's capacity to resonate with other ethnic heritages, nor does it preserve one's capacity to be fully moved by or stand in amazement before other heritages. At the same time, it must be conceded that we all have blind spots, we all "hit the wall" and reach for the ready answer. The question is how and where and with what consequences?

Martin Heidegger is another case of a superb thinker—a first-rate scholar who initially embarked on the awe-laden path.[23] He posited a spacious and revolutionary worldview, with stunning social and psychological implications. Yet this same pioneer who called for people to be "resolute" (faithful to their own inner callings), visionary (beyond the constraints of contemporary language and culture), and "open" to the "clearings" of being was also the man who identified himself with Hitler and later with the Nazification of German education.[24] On the eve of Hitler's election he wrote:

> What then is the nature of this event? The People is regaining the TRUTH of its will to existence [*dasein*], for truth is the manifestness [*offenbarkeit*] of that which makes a people sure, bright, and strong in action and knowledge. Out of such truth springs the genuine will to know…. Science [*wissenschaft*] is tied in with the necessity of the self-responsible existence [*dasein*] of the People. Scientific endeavor, thus is the pedagogic passion for wanting to know in order to convey knowledge. To *have* knowledge, however, means to master things with clarity and to be resolved to act.[25]

Returning to our inquiry then: How is it that such broadminded thinkers as Jung and Heidegger get knocked off center, as it were, whereas others, such as Tillich and Jaspers who encountered similar historical forces, managed to retain their cen-

ters? How is it that a *Mein Kampf,* written years before Hitler's
ascension to power and a virtual billboard for fascistic political
principles, could be minimized by the likes of Jung and Heidegger
or, for that matter, so many of Europe's intelligentsia? How could
Nazi thuggery—amply demonstrated by the early 1930s—go unchallenged by these trailblazers? How is it that a liberal mind like
Sartre could embrace Stalinist communism—even transitional-
ly—whereas his compatriot Camus refused any such cavorting?[26]
These are questions that must be posed. It is particularly important for those of us who philosophically resonate to Heidegger,
Jung, and Sartre to respond to the conundrum they present, for if
the most liberated minds go astray, where does this leave the rest
of us? What lesson does this leave the rest of us?

My guess is that we would find the answer to the aforementioned in the familial and cultural wounds that we carry and in
our failure to redress those wounds. Indeed, in the case of both
Heidegger and Jung, we find that repressive parenting punctuated
their family histories.[27] Both Heidegger and Jung's fathers, for example, were conservative ministers, and they both incited rebellion
in their independence-minded sons. Both also associated with
paternal mentors, Husserl in the case of Heidegger, and Freud in
the case of Jung. Whereas these mentors were not religious per se,
they were exceedingly authoritative, and represented in their own
distinctive ways the Jewish half of the Judeo-Christian heritage.
This coincidence of relationships, in my view, led Heidegger and
Jung to a profound rejection of the conventionally religious, the established, and the institutional. It further led to an intense cynicism
about Western cultural mores and the post-Enlightenment world.
Close on the heals of this inner turmoil, moreover, was the outer
turmoil of World War I, post-Versailles Germany, and the Great
Depression. The confluence of these factors on Heidegger and
Jung, and particularly for intellectuals who staked their beliefs on
Enlightenment rationalism, industrialization, and human progress,
could not be overestimated. They were staggering. In 1914, the very
notion of progress was exploded, and the world reeled in response.
Such were the staging grounds, not merely for fervent outbreaks

of creativity, but for demonic cults, sadists, and demagogues.[28] The blow to modern vanity, then, to the belief in human civility, was pervasive. Early Nazism epitomized this blow. Its occultism, ethnocentrism, and absolutism were all holdovers from a pre-industrial age. Hitler, too, was a holdover in many ways—the very antithesis of the measured, the rational, and the civil.

Particularly in the early years, Hitler and Nazism had a certain appeal to disaffected intellectuals. They embodied a *geist* or spirit—some would say frenzy—that directly challenged the faltering Enlightenment vision. By revolting against nineteenth century individualism, materialism, and scientism, Nazi ideology fancied itself as a spiritual antidote to the latter. The great irony, of course, is that in order to impose its ill-fated romanticism, Nazism itself was riveted with Enlightenment excesses, e.g., technocratization, automatism, and militarism. Still, like many, Jung and Heidegger appeared to be susceptible to National Socialism's mystique. Enlightenment rationality and Judeo-Christian morality had decisively capsized, in their view, and a fresh alternative was necessary. But again, was *Nazism* the "fresh" alternative? Where was the discernment? Where was the follow-through from their own inclusivist worldviews? It was lost in a hurt, a hurt that sought and temporarily found an Answer. But what the hurt really needed was more questions, a searching dialogue, and time.

The best of the emancipatory thinkers attended to these ministrations, even when they transiently found answers. In the most adverse circumstances, moreover, they challenged themselves, faced and held the tension, and refused to settle for the "near-at-hand." Martin Luther King, Jr., who was influenced by Tillich, for example, writes: "growth comes through struggle.... I decided early to give my life to something eternal and absolute. Not to these little gods that are here today and gone tomorrow. But to God who is the same yesterday, today, and forever."[29] Mahatma Gandhi, who also influenced King, adds, "truth is not to be found by anybody who has not got an abundant sense of humility. If you would swim on the bosom of the ocean of truth, you must reduce yourself to a zero."[30] He goes on: "I hold that complete realization is impossible in this embodied life. Nor is it necessary. A living immovable faith is all that is required for reaching the full spiritual height attainable by human beings."[31] To be sure, inquirers such as Gandhi, King, Tillich, Camus, and Jaspers all had their flaws. Like each of us, they all buckled under at certain points and caved in to their deficits. But the results of their transgressions were delimited—they must be looked at in the greater context of those inquirers' lives and the lives of those about them. Of course, the same could be said, and has been argued, about Heidegger, Jung, and Sartre. But I contend that with the aforementioned— and Heidegger in particular—the transgressions were of such a magnitude that little could support their justification.[32]

The Present Challenges of Faith: Magnificence, Mystery, and Responsibility

What, then, is our present task? How is it that *we* can preserve our centers and sustain a faith in the inscrutable? Before we respond to this question, let us first review what such a faith implies. Faith in the inscrutable associates with three intertwining dimensions: the magnificence of creation, the mystery or obscurity of creation, and our responsibility or ability to respond to creation.

Magnificence

The inscrutable implies magnificence as well as mystery; faith in the inscrutable implies faith in the magnificent. One of life's primary allures is the magnificence of creation. While there are other allures—bodily delights, pleasures of mind—the magnificence of creation is at their font.

That creation exists at all is magnificent; and no dimension is exempt—neither the small nor the great, the bereft nor the luxuriant, the obscure nor the indubitable. The span of humanity's hope matches precisely the reach of magnificence. While hope can be experienced in the absence of such vastness—as tough-minded materialists are wont to remind us—I question such hope's resiliency, intensity, and durability. I also question its validity. What does it take to perceive creation's magnitude? A breath?

The magnificence of creation demands tolerance—unbridled openness. Death informs life and life illuminates death. Winter storms bring spring blossoms, and darkness accentuates light. It is all great before the banquet of life, and no individual piece can stand for the whole, or render it diminished.

Whitman puts it this way:

> Great is goodness; I do not know what it is any more than I know what health is…. but I know it is great. Great is wickedness…. I find I often admire it just as much as I admire goodness: Do you call that a paradox? It certainly is a paradox.

> The eternal equilibrium of things is great, and the eternal overthrow of things is great, And there is another paradox.
> Great is life…and real and mystical…wherever and whoever.
> Great is death….Sure as life holds all parts together, death holds all parts together; Sure as the stars return again after they merge in the light; death is great as life. [33]

He goes on,

> Grand is the seen, the light of me—grand are the sky and stars,
> Grand is the earth, and grand are lasting time and space,
> And grand their laws, so multiform, puzzling, evolutionary;
> But grander far the unseen soul of me, comprehending and endowing all those,
> Lighting the light, the sky and stars,
> delving the earth, sailing the sea,
> (What were all those, indeed, without thee unseen soul?
> Of what amount without thee?)
> More evolutionary, vast, puzzling, O my soul!
> More multiform far—more lasting thou than they.[34]

Mystery

The flipside of magnificence is mystery. Being is mystery, and so is nonbeing. They are great, but they are fathomless. Mystery implies anxiety, but it also implies poignancy, depth, and possibility. Faith in the inscrutable invokes both magnificence and mystery, hope and uncertainty. As Whitman implies, we cannot have magnificence without uncertainty, and we cannot have mystery without hope. This paradox is sometimes overlooked in mystical/transpersonal circles.

"Here the limit of mysticism becomes visible," writes Tillich. "[I]t neglects the human predicament and the separation of man from the ultimate. There is no faith without separation."[35]

But with separation comes unsettlement, and faith must live with unsettlement. Unsettlement reminds us of our fragility, but it also reminds us of our possibility. Without separation, we are complete, inert; with separation, we are in search. Without separation we are at every moment who we are, consummated; with separation we are at every moment who we are not, evolving.

Again Tillich:

> For man is finite, and he can never unite all elements of truth in complete balance. On the other hand, he cannot rest on the awareness of his finitude, because faith is concerned with the ultimate and its adequate expression. Man's faith is inadequate if his whole existence is determined by something that is less than ultimate. Therefore, he must always try to break through the limits of his finitude and reach what never can be reached, the ultimate itself.[36]

Responsibility

Linked with mystery is responsibility, the challenge to respond. It is precisely out of uncertainty that we are called to responsibility. Whereas conventional faith downplays the role of uncertainty, faith in the inscrutable faces it head on. But what does it mean to face uncertainty head on? It means that individuals (as opposed to outside authorities) must bear the brunt of decision-making, but it also means that there is a dimension beyond which individuals are able to make decisions. Let us look more closely at this conundrum.

The burden of individual responsibility, the ability to respond, is echoed directly by creation's impenetrability. Within this opaqueness, there is no marked path, no "highway to heaven," and no inviolable canon. By contrast, it is *we* who must struggle with the inviolability, *we* who must sanctify the scripts. As Becker suggested, there is a formidable gap between the reflexive and reflective (or dialectical) approaches to worship. The former, characterized by doctrinal religious practice, readily subordinates the self, passively defers to authority, and seamlessly melds with others. The latter, on the other hand, engages with self, grapples with authority, and exchanges with others.[37] Whereas both doctrinal and dialectical forms of faith submit to higher powers, the question is how and with what degree of discernment? As noted earlier by Becker, dialectical faith promotes a stodgy surrender, a giving up "when there's nothing left," and a trust in the "tremendous creative energies" of the universe. Anything short of that for Becker is suspect. Similarly, faith in the inscrutable advocates the maximal mobilization of self, the furthest searches into life, and the fullest participation in living, prior to wholesale prostration. The questions for each individual at each interval are: How readily are you going to go down? How willing are you to live? With whom or for what are you willing to live?

In sum, our responsibility is to magnificence as well as to mystery—to hope in doubt as well as to doubt in hope. To live short of these is to live short of our birthright and to settle for palliatives. Inscrutability *is* magnificent; it is also mysterious. The question is whether we can step up to this predicament? Can we stay open to its intensity—at home, in our schools, and at our jobs—or will we continue to partialize, trivialize, or ignore its effects?

9

From Spirit to Society

The beginning of our happiness lies in the understanding that life without wonder is not worth living. What we lack is not a will to believe but a will to wonder.

—Abraham Heschel (*Man is not alone: A philosophy of religion*, New York: Farrar, Straus & Giroux, 1951, p. 37)

The social transformation heralded by faith in the inscrutable is foundation-shaking. In the quaver of such a world, for example, science would interface with religion, and religion with science. There would be a radically new approach to technology. While acknowledging technology's magnificence—from genetics to medicine to electronics—there would be an equal recognition of its banality. Organs without organismic purpose, medications without motivations, and data bases without wisdom would provide cold comfort to questing lives. Likewise, while acknowledging technology's mystery, wonder, and evolving nature, there would be an equal recognition of its delimits in these areas. A critical eye would be cast toward science and technology's tendency to doubt everything but itself, to perceive the unknown as a vast technical puzzle which will someday be deduced. There would be a new consciousness in science about inquiries that transcend the measurable and that open to the literary, metaphorical, and aesthetic. The method of controlled scientific inquiry would be supplemented by intuitive, poetic, and kinesthetic modes of investigation, contingent on questions asked and aims pursued. [1]

Equally, there would be a recognition on the part of religion that it too is fallible, that the magnificence of churches and holy books can be complemented by artificial hearts and superconductors, and that piety does not necessarily resolve scarcity, poverty, or calamity—but people can. There would be an acknowledgment of the limits of institutionalization and dogma in religious life, which often serve to subvert rather than ennoble religious causes. Correspondingly, there would be a recognition of the limits of religious inquiry. While aspects of such inquiry are legitimated by official religious doctrine, rarely are they pursued to their fuller and more radical implications. To the contrary, they are often muted, sanitized, or theologically defanged. Examples of this predilection abound, as in, for instance, the traditional interpretation of the biblical story of Job. In this classic rendering, Job (like everyperson) is a helpless victim of God's seeming arbitrariness. For no apparent reason, goes the story, Job is subjected to illness, loss, and upheaval; yet, as traditionalists (and God Himself in the story) hope, he steadfastly maintains his faith. The story, we are told, is precisely about such piety, regardless of the tragedy that befalls one. Moreover, it is about God "working in mysterious ways," but ultimately for our good, if we are good and adhere to His supposed commands. The catch here, however, is not so much that God is mysterious—which is downplayed by traditionalists—but that no matter how people are tested, they should adhere to God's (that is, doctrinal) commands. As traditionally conceived, then, the Job story is less about arbitrariness than about obedience, loyalty, and canonical conformity! The story, of course, could (and has) been read very differently.[2] A more existential rendering would have Job acknowledging God (or creation) as a transcendent power, but without the prescriptive requirement (e.g., biblical canon) that is conventionally attached to such an acknowledgment. Moreover, in the absence of such a requirement, Job would struggle himself with the moral implications of his "test," and *he*, in turn, would be responsible for its outcome.

In such a world, then, science and religion would complement each other. Where investment in the visible world (science) might falter, for example, consideration of the invisible world (religion) could rejuvenate; and where dogma (religion) may hinder; evidence-building (science) could unveil. On the other hand, where evidence-building (science) may hinder, intuition (religion) could illuminate; and where one domain might recoil, the other could dare, and so on.

The result of such an interplay would be nothing less than revolutionary for both science and religion. Each would be fortified by the other's magnificence and humbled before the other's mystery. Society, too, would benefit from the complementarity—as deeper questions would be probed and broader answers supplied.

What then do we know of the contemporary challenge? We know that magnificence and mystery are fundamental. Without magnificence, hope flags, and in the absence of mystery, depth, poignancy, and sensitivity wane. We also know that neither the jigsaw puzzle universe of science nor the narrow sectarianism of religion can uphold magnificence and mystery. Neither can sustain the grandeur, radiance, or doubt of the human predicament; and both can serve ultimately to flatten, pacify, and alienate. We cannot flourish in such a world; we cannot soar. Duties would usurp passions; analysis, sensibility; and systematization, discovery.

On the other hand, "anything goes" libertinism is also not the answer. Magnificence devolves into a routine within such a context; and mystery deteriorates into whimsy. There is precious little pausing in such a world; centering and sacralizing are cast aside. All, by contrast, becomes a jumble, a jolt, and a charge—stimulation without form, activation without purpose, feeling without commitment.

In short, faith in the inscrutable reaches far into hope but without canceling doubt; it keeps questions open, fluid, but it also recognizes fate and circumstance. These dynamics play out as follows: Where magnificence intoxicates, mystery sobers; where mystery perturbs, magnificence soothes. On the other hand, where magnificence withers, mystery renews, and where mystery depletes, magnificence restores.

There are many vehicles by which faith in the inscrutable—the magnificence and mystery of creation—can be lived out. Among the more exemplary are: intra- and interpersonal love, sexuality, art, meditation, and athleticism. Also included are the awe-based vocational and educational visions to which I have alluded. But faith in the inscrutable is not formulaic; it does not mandate a particular calling, vocation, or direction. What it does suggest, however, is a *spirit* (conducive to some paths more than others, to be sure) that can inform and revitalize.

The real questions are: How much does one absorb magnificence and mystery into one's daily practices, and how do magnificence and mystery play out in the practices of one's culture?

The future of humanity hinges on the latter question, for the future—like no other time in history—will depend on boldness and constraint, courage and humility. Consider, for example, the likely social composition of late-twenty-first-century life. Less and less will peoples of the world maintain their respective isolation, and increasingly they will coalesce. There will be increasing numbers of racially mixed friendships, interfaith marriages, and ethnically blended families. In America, for example, late-twenty-first-century-life is likely to look more like present-day San Francisco than present-day Chicago. Increasingly, we will observe offspring of mixed heritage—Asian and Caucasian, Hispanic and African, Arab and Indian, and so on. No longer will one be able to draw simple lines around people's ethnic, racial, and even sexual orientations, and less and less will people be able to identify with one pervasive lineage. By contrast, the people of the late-twenty-first-century will grope with a menagerie of inheritances—moral, religious, and political—often within single individuals; and they will face diverse and multiple directions by which to lead their lives. Progressively, the power that was once accorded solely to God, or the State, or the Institution, will now rest with ordinary mortals—and there will be dwindling standards to which these mortals will unquestioningly cling.[3]

Couple the diversification of society with that of emerging technology and the challenges become plainer. Late-twenty-first-century life, for example, is likely to be a distinctively synthetic life. Drugs will supplant moods, genetic codes will redesign bodies, and manufactured realities will eclipse those that are naturally given. But that is not all; among the other emerging and potential shifts heralded by late-twenty-first-century life, consider the following:

Archeology and anthropology are poised to open unprecedented frontiers of understanding—from fresh revelations about the beliefs and practices of pre-historic peoples to novel insights concerning Eastern and Western rapprochement.

Astronomers and physicists should give us dizzying glimpses of the microcosm and macrocosm—the origins of matter, the composition of life, and the rudiments of space-time.

Psychologists, neuroscientists, and philosophers are likely to make notable inroads into the investigation of consciousness. There are likely to be luminous revelations about the mutability and roots of our identities: our capacity to evolve new identities, to transcend old or outworn identities, and to deepen existing identities.[4] There should be groundbreaking elucidations of dream states, hallucinations, out-of-body experiences, and telepathic phenomena that should spur novel experimentation. That which once seemed fringe or irrational may soon be accepted as possible and inherent, such as the elucidation of body memories, the articulation of neural (somatic) "nets," and the elaboration of psychic fields.[5] And if we carry the expansion far enough, we may learn about our identifications with the remotest planes of our incarnation, from the one-celled germ plasm to the atomic and perhaps even subatomic noösphere (or sphere of mind). We may illuminate a consciousness that only mystics or—from a dimmer standpoint, psychotics—have observed and reported. This consciousness could include identity diffusions of an unprecedented scope, including expansions that link us to virtually every known element across countless temporal planes. Talk about magnificence and mystery! Just think what these discoveries could mean in terms of historical understanding, intra- and interpersonal connectedness, and environmental appreciation.

But we are still a long way from such world-shifts. We should fathom them, but not become swept up by them. Our freshest energies, on the other hand, must be reserved for present challenges.

Faith in the Inscrutable as a Present Task

Not unlike its spiritual forerunners, faith in the inscrutable provides an anti-authoritarian reply to the present difficulties. As we shall see, this reply is flexible, situational, and considered. It is also, on the other hand, modestly less consoling—and palpably more disquieting—than that of its predecessors.

For example, Buddhism corresponds very closely to faith in the inscrutable. The Buddhist precepts of openness, appreciation, and discernment resonate acutely with the precepts of magnificence, mystery, and responsibility; and the Buddhist ideal of maximal disidentification, selfless right action, and godless piety, are all values that echo a fluid center and existential faith.[6] The difference however is in the purity of these values. Whereas Buddhism—at least as it has become institutionalized—attributes a clarity, incisiveness, and lawfulness to its precepts, the faith I present here is appreciably less assured. Compare, for example, the following two passages that reflect the respective positions. In the first, Conze outlines the Buddhist conceptions of Nirvana and Godhead; in the second, Tillich introduces his notion of sanctification (or New Being), which emerges from existential faith. Conze writes:

> Nirvana is permanent, stable, imperishable, immovable, ageless, deathless, unborn, and unbecome…it is power, bliss, and happiness, the secure refuge, the shelter, and the place of unassailable safety;…it is the real Truth and the supreme Reality;…it is the Good, the supreme goal and the one and only consummation of our life, the eternal, hidden, and incomprehensible Peace.[7]

Tillich, on the other hand, proposes:

> Sanctification includes awareness of the demonic as well as of the divine. Such awareness, which increases in the process of sanctification, does not lead to the stoic "wise man," who is superior to the ambiguities of life because he has conquered his passions and desires, but rather to an awareness of these ambiguities in himself, as in everyone, and to the power of affirming life and its vital dynamics in spite of its ambiguities.[8]

From these passages, it may now be clear how *lack* of assurance in the existential paradigm is both potentially freeing and potentially limiting. For it is precisely this lack that loosens the hermeneutic circle, keeps questions alive, and prods people to their edge. To the degree that it can be supplemented with courage, lack of assurance can alert us to coming dangers, stretch us toward fresh horizons, and apprise us of timely opportunities. Overconfidence, on the other hand, can promote the opposite tendencies—rigidity, complacency, and inertia. While the Buddhist perspective is not arguably overconfident, it does infer consolations—states of "bliss," "selflessness," etc.—that a *fluid* center (not to mention the Buddha himself, perhaps) would challenge. On the other hand, the kinship between the respective worldviews is notable, and the differences are a matter of nuance more than category. Would the practical consequences of following the respective worldviews diverge? I suspect so, but the evidence for this development has yet to be appreciably demonstrated.

The Ethical Task

Tillich describes the moral principle of *agape* (or loving self-sacrifice), as "the 'star' above the chaos of relativism."[9] The problem, he goes on, is that under the ambiguities and conditions of existence, we need "more than one star to guide us."[10] His caveat holds for faith in the inscrutable as well. While the maintenance of a fluid center between magnificence and mystery is an exalted starting point, it does not flesh out what a woman should do if she has an unwanted pregnancy, or how a homicide victim's family ought to react to the perpetrator, or how a spouse should deal with a philandering partner, or, in the case of more common occurrences, what kind of romantic partner a person should court, what level of ethical violation one should accept at work, how much television one should watch, or how much alcohol one should consume. Moreover, these issues do not even approach the emerging challenges of how to respond to fundamentalist religion, overpopulation, and global terrorism.

Yet, there are mooring points in all this puzzlement, inner guideposts. To begin with, faith in the inscrutable implies a "listening love," as Tillich puts it, which takes us beyond either stock reactions or reckless willfulness. "Listening love," elaborates Tillich, "is a listening to and looking at the concrete situation in all its concreteness, which includes the deepest motives of the other person."[11] He goes on to point out that this form of inquiry has particular advantages in the modern world, with the recent insights into individual and social psychology, cultural dynamics, and biology. Yet listening love is not merely an intellectual tactic; it is a discipline that requires profound *presence*.

As the reader may recall, presence is an integral aspect of depth psychotherapy; yet it is also central to moral and ethical domains. This is because presence reaches beyond the merely cognitive and immerses the seeker in the sensibilities of his or her affect, body, and imagination. With the intricacies of presence, one discovers the resonances to one's possible course of action, and not merely its proscribed or predictable features. One is challenged to come alive in the context of presence—to sense, feel, and deliberate—and not merely to stand by. Mature spirituality, Tillich elaborates, is a creative synthesis. It considers both the received wisdom of the past and the evolving wisdom of the present; above all, he goes on, it alerts one to the enormity of one's undertaking.[12]

It is precisely this enormity—the magnificence and mystery of creation—that any profound decision must confront. One must see it in the unborn child, but also in the unborn potential of the child's bearer, in the "life" that is the embryo, but also in the life that the embryo will face. It must be perceptible in the face of a victim, but also, at some level of communality, in the gaze of a victimizer. It must be evident in the spurned lover, but also, correspondingly, in the lover who strayed. It must even be detectable in our technological revolutions, but also, equally, in our steadfast resistance to those revolutions. The point is that if we are to respond with depth, attunement, and embodiment, then we will need to engage with as many sides of a problem as possible.

We will need to immerse ourselves in the ambiguity if we are to emerge with conviction, intention, and integrity. Again Tillich: "The more seriously one has considered all the factors involved in a moral decision, the absolute as well as the relative factors, the more one can be certain that there is a power of acceptance in the depth of life," and in our own lives for the decision we risk.[13]

The net effect of such awe-based deliberation may someday be momentous. Decreasingly, decisions would be mediated through commandment, norm, or whim, and increasingly they would be filtered through contemplation, empathy, and distillation. While listening love, faith in the inscrutable, and magnificence and mystery cannot map out a blueprint for a revitalized world, they provide key glimpses of how such a world might unfold.

These glimpses suggest a comparatively flexible, experimental world, a world in which there will be much more boundary-crossing—ethnic, religious, and sexual—but also, and not to be discounted, biological and bio-technical. Laws and traditions are likely to be respected in such a world, perhaps even more so than today, but there will be an equal emphasis on the evolving and individual case. Decisions will be more deliberative, heartfelt, and embodied, and, as a result, both more reticent and adventurous. Decisions will be more reticent, for example, because there will be a greater sensitivity to unwelcome boundary-crossings, such as rash exploitations of genetics, robotics, or mind-altering drugs. While "progress" in these areas will go on, it will be notably more scrutinized than is currently the case, and, hence, more carefully controlled. On the other hand, many decisions are likely to become more daring than they are today, particularly if we can avert a world crisis. For example, people will be inclined to take more risks with their careers, hobbies, and leisure activities. Travel will become more of an adventure—a flight or trek to a remote part of the world—or an integral part of one's day-to-day life. People will experiment more with alternative lifestyles—such as rethinking their roles as isolated individuals, expanding their gender and vocational potentials, and deepening their commitments to children. There will be a diminishing reliance on the quick, the easy, and the fashionable, and a balder acknowledgment of the beckoning, the deepening, and the enduring.

The thrust of this reformation will be an enhanced appreciation for our fullness, our greatness, before the engagement with life. But it will also be a strengthened respect for our fragility in certain areas and for our needs to rein in. We will be the beneficiaries of centuries of wisdom-teachings about the plasticity of our selves, and, as suggested earlier, the necessity to live out that plasticity.[14] Moreover, we will realize that the more we live out the various parts of ourselves, the more we can clarify, distill, and amplify the kind of selves we desire to be. The poignant paradox here will not be lost on us—that the further we participate in "other" realities, the more we deepen our own, at least to a point. Here lies the greatness of Nietzsche, James, Freud, Jung, and all those frontierspeople who recognized humanity's range.

We are knots of relation, as Merleau-Ponty intimated, who weave and wend our way through stretches of space, enormities of time, and labyrinths of imagination.[15] We are beasts and trees and meadows; and we are worms and wastes and winds. This is our horrifying problem and our electrifying promise. Soon, or at least not as remotely as we might think, we may be able to tap these dizzying sensibilities, and not just through drugs or robotics, but through outbreaks of awe, surges of connectedness, and flares of vision.

But we must not be naïve about this revolutionary prospect; the harrowing potential for post-structural malaise, confusion, and even anarchy must not simply be dismissed. Even today, these potentialities loom, and they will trail us persistently.

Hence, the question is how to be smart about this coming transformation; how to be responsive toward rather than reactive about its singular demands?

We can start in this direction by acknowledging our limitedness. While the prospect of liberating untold potential for experience is seductive, we must not simply yield to it. We must recognize that a surfeit of identities cannot be simultaneously assimilated, and that to promote cohesion, there must be a modicum of discretion, safety, and presence. Moreover, it is difficult enough to negotiate the differences within native backgrounds or cultures, let alone those that are at variance. Wisdom dictates that we approach identity changes with sobriety, that we "dwell" in their implications, and that we prioritize them with care. While such precautionary notions may at times seem oppressive, they are fundamental for substantive, integrative change. Capricious encounters with otherness, on the other hand, promote capricious consciousness—cosmetic insights, confused motives, and aimless actions. Examples of the former can be found in the "true believer" syndrome, where individuals will flock from sect to sect, person to person, and experience to experience, not for the realization of consciousness but for the avoidance of depth, commitment, and discipline.[16]

The upshot here is to reckon with magnificence and mystery, for if they are not in one's deliberations, they are not likely to be in one's resolutions, and if they are not in one's resolutions, then a mournful life will likely result. Magnificence and mystery are crucial mooring points, key touchstones in the encounter with life. To the degree we are mindful of them—as well as their absence—our decisions are likely to be, if not inviolable, then dignified. Their dignity derives from our having deeply inquired, roundly searched, and ardently risked. That is the best we humans can offer, the most courageous and forward-looking that we can be.

10

Glimmerings: Enchanted Agnosticism and the Future

Tell me, what is it you plan to do with your one wild and precious life?

—Mary Oliver (*House of light*, Boston: Beacon Press, 1990, p. 60)

I envision a time when the spiritual philosophy of faith in the inscrutable, that which I call *enchanted agnosticism*, becomes the norm.

Enchantment and agnosticism have a long and many-layered history. Enchantment has traditionally been associated with religion (wonder, magic), whereas agnosticism has been linked with science (doubt, skepticism).[1] Yet religion and science are not necessarily antagonists, and, as this volume has proposed, can be advocates, collaborators in an enlarged mission.

By *enchanted* agnosticism, then, I mean an agnosticism that revels in and does not merely tolerate mystery, an agnosticism that legitimates passion and countenances faith; but equally, and with equal fervor, an agnosticism that humbles, questions, and revises, as well as enchants!

Taken together, I view *enchanted agnosticism* as bedazzled uncertainty, exhilarated discernment, and enraptured curiosity; it is the openness and skepticism of science wedded to the zeal and exaltation of religion; and it is the veneration of mystery wedded to the solemnity of responsibility.

Further, I view enchanted agnosticism as a radical new life-philosophy: it is a view that trumps nihilism as it does dogma, purposelessness as it does certitude. It is a view that basks not in particular things, but in the amazement and astonishment *of* things. It does not matter what you call this existence—God or

Spirit or Nature—but what does matter is that it is incredible, however conceived.

More formally, I define enchanted agnosticism in terms of the following three suppositions: that the source of the universe (e.g., God, quanta) is unknown; that this unknown is amazing and awe-inspiring, as well as daunting and overwhelming; and that people need to respond to (i.e., take responsibility for) rather than react against this paradoxical condition.

In her illuminating study of religion—*A History of God*—Karen Armstrong concludes that we in the West have reached a developmental milestone. We have witnessed the disasters of fundamentalist tyrannies, and equally, of post-Enlightenment oligarchies, and we are in need of something different. This alternative, Armstrong suggests, just might be what she calls "mystical agnosticism," which is very akin to my "enchanted agnosticism." The problem, however, Armstrong cautions, is that in order for such an alternative to be viable, it must be "felt upon the pulse," or, as Buber put it, "hallowed in the everyday." This is precisely the challenge that I pose here: to feel enchanted agnosticism upon the pulse.[2]

How then are we to *live* enchanted agnosticism, and where will it be felt upon our pulse? While I leave the essence of this question to the reader, allow me to muse a moment:

I envision a time when enchanted agnosticism is echoed in schools and in temples, in boardrooms and in embassies, and in bedrooms and in alleyways—in every human sphere. This would be a time when churches throw open their doors to mosques, and mosques to synagogues, when Buddhist priests can perform sacred chanting rites before Hindu congregants, and when Jewish temples sanction Protestant services. It would be a time, perhaps, when every major denomination will regularly and on a rotating basis host every other major denomination, and yet maintain their respective identities. It would be a time when families of all faiths and backgrounds will pray together, break bread together, and behold the mystery and marvels of each others' heritages.

I envision a time when enchanted agnosticism—awe-based living—is practiced in business and diplomatic circles and when politicians and mediators and entrepreneurs *model* the actions they expect of others, when they partake in interfaith ceremonies, when they avail themselves to intimate interchange and when they open themselves to diverse folk traditions. Then, and only then will the spirals of hate, of tit for tat, and of intercultural estrangement be stanched. Then and only then will conciliation have a chance.

Respect, here, is key. Although hard-core or extremist types would probably resist this respect—and might even violently oppose it due to the threat it poses to their rigidity—numerous others, including those who might otherwise have become extreme, would take a different stance. This stance would be one of curiosity, wonderment, and, potentially, even attraction. Commensurate with the rise in enchanted agnosticism would be the corresponding rise in intra- and intercultural reassessment, trust, and cooperation. With these developments, entire worlds will unfurl. Religious and scientific types, for example, will begin to perceive not only their respective divergences, but also their respective convergences, usefulnesses, and virtues. While adherents of doctrinal faith will reassess the value of openness and skepticism, devotees of calculation will reevaluate the legitimacy of veneration and faith. While spiritualists will rethink material realities, materialists will revisit the ethereal, poetic, and felt. Although hesitant at first, each of the respective parties would become increasingly appreciative of the others' legitimacy, lucidity, and sublimity.

I envision a time when diplomatic and trade meetings are attended not only by policymakers, but also by ethical philosophers, spiritual leaders, and organizational psychologists; when, for example, attendees participate in professionally facilitated process groups, and promote frank exchanges of feeling, and when the input from scientists and philosophers matches that from legislators and generals. I envision a time when representatives can broach each others' personal fears as well as state or corporate agendas; when international relations can be spoken about in terms of interpersonal relations; and when hopes and trepidations can be coupled with predictions and averages.

One vision I have here is the formation of a gestalt-like

group as a component of legislative procedure. Why shouldn't senators and state representatives meet with each other in professionally facilitated encounter groups as a part of their deliberative processes—particularly when major ethical issues are at stake? Just consider, for example, how a senator (or a secretary of state or a president for that matter!) investigating the need for war in a remote land might be impacted by a frank and emotionally disclosing encounter with a fellow senator—or with witnesses—testifying both on behalf of and against war. Consider how informative such an engagement might be, and not just in the formulation of strategy, but in the formulation of an enlarged and balanced view.[3]

Do these musings sound remote or hopelessly out-of-reach? I do not believe so, and neither did social theorists such as Carl Rogers who have been promoting such interchanges for years.[4] For example, at a 1985 conference of international leaders—co-sponsored by Rogers' Center for the Study of the Person and the University for Peace (Costa Rica)—a heated discussion ensued about the state of U.S.-Nicaraguan relations. Reflecting on the results of that discussion, a delegate from Nicaragua commented:

> I am convinced that there *are* possibilities. Before coming here, I thought the same. But what got confirmed here is that a great power will listen to a small country, and *here* mistrust *has* been overcome.... The possibility *really* exists to solve problems in Central America.[5]

And another delegate declared:

> Thank you for a very important experience! I think the result of those four days is amazing, changing hostility to trust. I do wish your method will be used in many peace efforts.... For me personally your way of meeting me I think will change my life.[6]

At the same time, however, we must be circumspect about such developments, particularly in the wake of September 11, 2001. Enchantment cannot flower without security; openness cannot flourish without stability. Just as in one-on-one relationships, safeguards in community will be essential, and particularly in awe-based environments. While many of these safeguards will arise naturally—from awe-based educational and vocational influences—some of them will have to be enforced. Nevertheless, these enforcements will be minimized, in my view, as polarization itself will be minimized.

As more partake in The Great Conversation, fewer will pine for The Great Detonation or The Holy Vindication. As some invite deepening and widening, others will permit risking and opening.

In short, enchanted agnosticism—the embrace of mystery—has tremendous potential to change our lives by addressing the confusion and spiritual hunger of our lives.

It holds humility at the same time as it accents risk-taking, and it provides an ethical consideration—listening love—that dwells on the interplay of humility and risk-taking.

Coda

In his timely critical essay, *The twilight of American culture*, Morris Berman quotes fellow essayist E.M. Forster. This quote is of particular relevance to the question before us: What sort of groups or individuals will lead us in the fight against polarization and how broadly will that leadership impact society? Forster answers with an allegory: "I believe in aristocracy," he opines,

> …. Not an aristocracy of power, based on rank and influence, but an aristocracy of the sensitive, the considerate, and the plucky. Its members are to be found in all nations and classes, and all through the ages, and there is a secret understanding between them when they meet. They represent the true human tradition, the one permanent victory of our queer race over cruelty and chaos…. On they go—an invincible army, yet not a victorious one. The aristocrats, the elect, the chosen, the

Best People—all the words that describe them are false, and all attempts to organize them fail. Again and again Authority, seeing their value, has tried to net them and to utilize them as the Egyptian Priesthood or the Christian Church or the Chinese Civil Service or the Group Movement, or some other worthy stunt. But they slip through the net and are gone; when the door is shut, they are no longer in the room; their temple…is the Holiness of the Heart's imagination, and their kingdom, though they never possess it, is the wide-open world.[7]

A better, more poetic description of the enchanted agnostic, the fluidly centered, and the awe-inspired, I have yet to find. At the same time, however, I believe Forster overlooks something here—as does Berman in his compelling assent. The implication in Forster's phrase "aristocracy of the sensitive" is plain: The finest people are estranged, secretive, and remote, few in the mainstream can relate to them, and most will never try. But is this necessarily so? Is there not something myopic in Forster's view, something that will not countenance change?

I am not so sure about Forster's "aristocracy." I am not so sure that "sensitivity," "consideration," and "pluck" are the province of an elite handful—at least not an impermeable province.

If there is one point I would like to stress in this volume, it is that awe and the fluid center— "sensitivity," "consideration," and "pluck"—are *humanity's* challenge, and not the exclusivity of a clique. Humanity—you and I—have a choice: We can replicate our record of contempt, or we can reach for something fuller, nobler, and wider ranging; we can polarize into oblivion, or we can tap the aristocracy of our hearts, souls, and depths.

The challenge, once again, is ours. The means to meet it— within our sights.

Notes

Notes to Background

1.   From *The Norton Critical Edition, Faust,* W. Arndt (trans.). NY: Norton, 1976, p. 158, Lines 6272–73 (originally pub. 1832).

2.   Pick up any standardized text or journal in psychology and you will find volumes on learning, perception, memory, and statistics, but virtually nothing on "awe." For rare exceptions see D. Keltner and J. Haidt, "Approaching awe: A moral, spiritual, and aesthetic emotion," *Cognition and Emotion,* Vol. 17 (2003), 297–314; L. Sundararajan, "Religious awe: Potential contributions of negative theology to psychology, 'positive' or otherwise," *Journal of Theoretical and Philosophical Psychology,* Vol. 22 (2002), 174–197; and E. M. Stern and R. Marchesani, eds., "Awe and trembling: Psychotherapy of unusual states," *The Psychotherapy Patient,* Vol. 11, nos. 1–2 (1999).

Also of note are several related (allbeit academically neglected) volumes, M. Lerner's *Spirit matters: Global healing and the wisdom of the soul* (Charlottesville, VA: Hampton Roads, 2000); D.N. Elkins's *Beyond religion: A personal program for building a spiritual life outside the walls of traditional religion* (Wheaton, IL: Quest Books, 1998); M. Berman's *Reenchantment of the world* (New York: Bantam, 1984), J. Hillman's *Revisioning Psychology.* (New York: Harper and Row, 1975), T. Moore's *Care of the Soul.* (New York: HarperCollins, 1992), and last but not least, of course, W. James's *Varieties of Religious Experience.* (New York: The Modern Library, 1936/1902).

It is worthy of further note that in a related mainstream volume, the term "awe" is completely absent from the index. See B. Spilka, R.W. Hood, B. Hunsberger, and R. Gorsuch, *The psychology of religion: An empirical approach* (New York: Guilford, 2003). On the other hand, D.M. Wulff's *Psychology of religion: Classic and contemporary* (New York: Wiley, 1997) is a welcome departure because "awe" appears liberally in the index and is accorded a sustained and respectful presence.

3.   There is a certain casualness that characterizes elements of the postmodern academic community—an intellectual remove. Consider for example, the following statement from Ken Gergen in *The saturated self: Dilemmas of identity in contemporary life* (New York: Basic Books, 1991), p. 197: "To pray, to feel remorse, to express gratitude, to conduct business, to make a scientific discovery are all forms of cultural ritual—constructed forms of activity particular to cultures in given times and places."

Perhaps this is so for aspects of experiences such as those above, but is it so for human experience as a whole, which is what Gergen, in much of his book, implies? While certain—and perhaps most—human experiences can be reduced to culturally relative rituals (or "games," as Gergen also terms them), others are not so readily grasped. The experience of human intimacy, for example, or wonder or death, cannot simply be relegated to regional or cultural forms, in my view. To the contrary, they are experientially fuller, weightier, and more inclusive; they are resonant with the human body as the philosopher Maurice Merleau-Ponty might have put it, and not just a localized language. Awe in my view is also of that aforementioned realm, and maybe at its fulcrum.

What I advance here then is not that awe is some invariant human essence, but that it is a broadly shared, widely valued sensibility; and that it concerns our most intimate perceptions of life.

4.   B. Barber, *Jihad vs. McWorld: How the planet is both falling apart and coming together* (New York: Times Books, 1995). The prophetic nature of this thesis was vividly illustrated by two recent events—the collapse of the World Trade Towers and the collapse of confidence in financial markets in the wake of the Enron scandal.

Notes to Introduction

1.   See R. Otto, *The idea of the holy* (London: Oxford University Press, 1923/1950). Originally published in 1923). "Awe" is defined throughout this work on the basis of the definition provided. This definition is excerpted from *Webster's New Collegiate Dictionary* (Springfield, MA: Miriam-Webster, 1988).

It should be of further note, moreover, that the concept of awe has been wonderfully rounded out by two contemporary theologians: Abraham Heschel, with his notion of "radical amazement," and Matthew Fox, with his vision of "creation spirituality."

2.   By "odd" form of materialism, I mean psychology's persistent quest to ground its data on observable and measurable units. These units need not be material per se, but they draw on material principles. Consider for example, the use of the computer model as a basis on which to understand cognition. See C. Aanstoos, "Cognitive science and the technological revolution: A humanistic response," in K.J. Schneider, J.F.T. Bugental, and J.F. Pierson, *The handbook of humanistic psychology: Leading edges in theory, research, and practice* (Thousand Oaks, CA: Sage, 2001), 213–24.

3.   C. Trungpa, *Crazy wisdom* (Boston: Shambala, 1991).

Notes to Chapter One

1.   See J. Kramer and D. Alstad, *The guru papers: Masks of authoritarian power*

(Berkeley, CA: North Atlantic Books, 1993); also K.J. Schneider, "The deified self: A 'centaur' response to Wilber and the transpersonal movement," *Journal of Humanistic Psychology*, Vol. 27 (1987), 196–216; and K.J. Schneider, "Infallibility is so damn appealing: A reply to Ken Wilber," *Journal of Humanistic Psychology*, Vol. 29 (1989), 495–506.

2.   See Editor, "Wipe out stress, pain and anxiety: The right bodywork can do it all," *New Age*, September/October (1999).

Deepak Chopra, in *The seven spiritual laws of success* (Novato, CA: New World Library, 1993), 1–2, announces confidently: "I have outlined the steps to wealth consciousness based on a *true* understanding of the workings of nature....When this knowledge is incorporated in your consciousness, it will give you the ability to create *unlimited* wealth with *effortless* ease, and to experience *success* in *every* endeavor" (emphasis mine).

Ken Wilber, on the other hand, has toned down but not entirely eradicated his puritanical leanings. For example, in his latest explanation of what he terms "integral psychology," he places literary luminaries such as Thoreau and Whitman, along with documented saints, on "lower" spiritual levels than those he claims have attained "nondual" consciousness (or "union with the entire world of form..."). See K. Wilber, "Waves, streams, and states of self: An outline of integral psychology," *The Humanistic Psychologist*, Vol. 31, Nos. 2–3, (2003), 27–28, 32.

Now I do not begrudge either Wilber or Chopra for their genuinely helpful literary contributions—of which there are a number; however, it is writing such as that illustrated above, that is of grave concern to me, and should be, it seems to me, to any circumspect observer.

3.   See P. Tillich, *Dynamics of faith* (New York: Harper and Row, 1957).

4.   See also S. Koch, " 'Psychology' or 'the psychological studies?' " *American Psychologist*, Vol. 48 (1993), 902–904.

5.   See A. van Kaam, *Foundations of existential psychology* (Pittsburgh: Duquesne University Press, 1966).

6.   By "verify," I do not mean statistically "prove" or substantiate a given claim; by contrast, I mean something closer to discovering patterns or structures of a given phenomenon. While the latter stresses linear-causality (which, more often than not, I believe, leads to superficiality of findings); the former stresses plausibility (which, in principle at least, enables both fullness of disclosure and cross-case comparisons). For an elaboration see the section on qualitative research in K.J. Schneider, J.F.T. Bugental, and J.F. Pierson, eds., *The handbook of humanistic psychology* (see above Notes to Introduction, note 2).

Notes to Chapter Two

1.   Cited in M. Freidman, ed., *The Worlds of Existentialism*. (Atlantic Highlands, NJ: Humanities Press, 1991), p. 38.

2.   See, for example, the discussion of intrauterine embeddedness vs. disruption of embeddedness in E.G. Schachtel, *Metamorphosis* (New York: Basic Books, 1959). Consider also the struggle for prenatal identity and life in R.D. Laing, *The facts of life* (New York: Ballantine, 1976) and S. Grof, *The adventure of self-discovery* (Albany: State University of New York Press, 1987). Although controversial and speculative, works such as the above should not be dismissed out of hand. Increasing evidence (e.g., see note 8) indicates that many bases for psychophysiological development are laid down in prenatal experience.

3.   See R.D. Laing, *The divided self: An existential study in sanity and madness* (Middlesex, England: Penguin, 1969).

4.   See G. Bateson, D. Jackson, J. Haley, and J. Weakland, "Toward a theory of schizophrenia," *Behavioral Science*, Vol. 1 (1956), 251; R.D. Laing, H. Phillipson, and A. Lee, *Interpersonal perception* (New York: Harper and Row, 1966); M. McGoldrick and R. Gerson, *Genograms in family assessment* (New York: Norton, 1985); E. Tronick, "Emotions and emotional communication in infants," *American Psychologist*, Vol. 44, No. 2, (1989), 112–119; and K. Kendler, C. Bulik, J. Silberg, J. Hettema, J. Myers, and C. Prescott, "Childhood sexual abuse and adult psychiatric and substance use disorders in women: An epidemiological and Cotwin control analysis," *Archives of General Psychiatry*, Vol. 57, No. 10, (2000), 953–959.

5.   E.G. Schachtel, *Metamorphosis*. (See above Chapter Two, note 2.)

6.   For an elaboration on this developmental model, see K.J. Schneider, *The paradoxical self: Toward an understanding of our contradictory nature* (Amherst, NY: Prometheus/Humanity Books, 1999).

7.   See J. Royce, *Encapsulated man* (New York: D. Van Nostrand, 1964). For an elaboration of the consumerist deception, see H. Marcuse, *One-dimensional man: Studies in the ideology of advanced industrial society* (Boston: Beacon Press, 1964); E. Becker, *Denial of death* (New York: Free Press, 1973); and M. Berman, *The twilight of American culture* (New York: Norton, 2000).

8.   From James, H., ed. (1920). *The letters of William James*, Vol. II. Boston: Atlantic Monthly Press, pp. 253–54. (This letter is dated May 6, 1906 to W. Lutoslawski.)

9.   V. Guidano, "Constructivist psychotherapy: A theoretical framework," in R.

Neimeyer and M. Mahoney, eds., *Constructivism in psychotherapy* (Washington, DC: American Psychological Association Press, 1995), 98. On the "unfolding" of human experience, see J. Welwood in K.J. Schneider, J.F.T. Bugental, and J.F. Pierson, eds., "The unfolding of human experience: Psychotherapy and beyond." *The handbook of humanistic psychology*, 333–341 (see above Notes to Introduction, note 2). On the "developmental spiral," see also S. Kirschner, *The romantic origins of psychoanalysis: Individuation and integration in post-Freudian theory* (New York: Cambridge University Press, 1996), 83.

10.   There is an increasing empirical literature which supports the link between maternal psychophysiology and prenatal development. See, for example, T. Achenbach, *Developmental psychopathology* (New York: Wiley, 1982), 152–158; and V. McLoyd, "Socioeconomic disadvantage and child development," *American Psychologist*, Vol. 53, No. 2, (1998), 185–204, for reviews. By "route" I mean more than neural pathway, but the design of one's entire (psychophysiological) experience of a given event.

11.   See E. Erikson, *Childhood and society* (New York: Norton, 1963); T. Brazelton, *Neonatal behavioral assessment* (London: Spastics International Medical Publications, 1973); M. Mahler, F. Pine, and A. Bergman, *The psychological birth of the human infant* (New York: Basic Books, 1975); J. Piaget, *The development of thought: Equilibration of cognitive structures* (New York: Viking, 1977); and L. Kohlberg, "The cognitive developmental approach," in T. Lickona, ed., *Moral development and moral behavior* (New York: Brunner/Mazel, 1978).

12.   P. Cushman, *Constructing the self, constructing America: A cultural history of psychotherapy* (Reading, MA: Addison-Wesley, 1995).

13.   For an exception, see B. Vandenberg, "Is epistemology enough? An existential consideration of development,"*American Psychologist*, Vol. 46 (1991), 1278–1286.

14.   By "twisted strands " I do not mean that Toby's entire life-design has become defunct nor that he has become psychotic. He, like most anyone in his situation, has suffered a temporary shock that has warped and battered his sense of self. At the most basic levels he is still able to follow established routes and adapt to present demands.

15.   W. Blake, "Proverbs of hell," cited in G. Bataille, *Literature and evil*, trans. by A. Hamilton (New York: Marion Boyars, Ltd., 1985), 94.

16.   For a fuller explication of this thesis, see K.J. Schneider, *Horror and the holy: Wisdom-teachings of the monster tale* (Chicago: Open Court, 1993).

17.   While there may be more mental health facilities available today than in the past, it is doubtful whether they provide either the privacy or support that could be found in a variety of naturalistic settings in our pre-industrial past. See, for

example, M. Foucault, *Madness and civilization: A history of insanity in the age of reason*, trans. by R. Howard (New York: Vintage, 1965); and M. Berman, *The twilight of American culture* (see above Chapter Two, note 7) for an elaboration.

18.   Literally translated from the Greek, "odyssey" means "pain," both one's own and others. To undergo an odyssey (as in Homer's classic) is to undergo a trial, according to literary authorities, but the alternative is oblivion. See S.G. Nugent, *The uses of enchantment*, audiotape, course no. 201 (Springfield, VA: The Teaching Company, 1997).

19.   Chronicle staff, "Fair shooting spurs review of security: Richmond man arrested in July 4th rampage," *San Francisco Chronicle*, July 6, 1998, A-1.

20.   S. Sontag, *Styles of radical will* (New York: Picador, 2002), 71.

21.   From M. Shelley, *Frankenstein* (New York: Bantam, 1818/1981), 15.

22.   See R. Otto, *The idea of the holy* (see above Notes to Introduction, note 1).

23.   E.A. Poe, "Eleanora," in *The complete tales of Edgar Allan Poe* (New York: Crown, 1842/1981), 301–304.

24.   See D.K. Simonton, *Greatness* (New York: Guilford, 1994) and K.R. Jamison, *Touched by fire: Manic-depressive illness and the artistic temperament* (New York: Free Press, 1993).

25.   A.H. Maslow, *The psychology of science: A reconnaissance* (Chicago: Henry Regnery, 1966).

26.   See A. Miller, *The untouched key: Tracing childhood trauma in creativity and destructiveness* (New York: Doubleday, 1988) and G. O'Connell Higgens, *Resilient adults: Overcoming a cruel past* (San Francisco: Jossey-Bass, 1994).

27.   A. Miller, *The untouched key* (see above Chapter Two, note 26).

28.   G. O'Connell Higgens, *Resilient adults*(San Francisco: Jossey-Bass, 1994) and R. May, "The wounded healer," in K.J. Schneider and R. May, eds., *The psychology of existence: An integrative, clinical perspective* (New York: McGraw-Hill, 1995).

29.   See A. Maslow, *Toward a psychology of being* (New York: D. Van Nostrand, 1968), 140; M. Csikszentmihalyi, *Creativity: Flow and the psychology of discovery and invention* (New York: Harper Perennial, 1996); and G. O'Connell Higgens, *Resilient adults* (see above Chapter Two, note 26).

30.   For examples of such personalities, see K.R. Jamison, *Touched by fire* and D.K. Simonton, *Greatness* (for both, see above Chapter Two, note 24).

31. F. Nietzsche, *The portable Nietzsche*, trans. by W. Kaufmann (New York: Viking/Penguin, 1889/1982), 554.

32. From William Blake, *Selected Poetry*. "The Marriage of Heaven and Hell." (London: Penguin Books, 1988, p. 73).

33. For examples, see G. O'Connell Higgens, *Resilient adults* and D.K. Simonton, *Greatness* (see above Chapter Two, notes 26 and 24, respectively).

34. For more examples, see D.K. Simonton, *Greatness*.

35. For eloquent elaborations on this challenge see E. Becker, *Denial of death* (see above Chapter Two, note 7) and M.C. Bateson, *Composing a life* (New York: Atlantic Monthly, 1989).

36. See Ortega y Gasset, *Revolt of the masses* (New York: Norton, 1936/1960) and R. Otto, *The idea of the holy* (see above Notes to Introduction, note 1).

37. See A. Miller, *The untouched key* (see above Chapter Two, note 26) and D. Burston, *The wing of madness* (Boston: Harvard University Press, 1996).

38. D.K. Simonton, *Greatness* (see above Chapter Two, note 24) puts this case especially strongly.

39. See especially E. Levinas, *Totality and infinity: An essay on exteriority* (Pittsburgh: Duquesne University Press, 1969) and M. Buber, *I and thou,* trans. by R. G. Smith (New York: Scribner, 1958). Few have plumbed this terrain more eloquently.

40. Informed readers will recognize a similarity between centeredness and fluidity and Jean Piaget's principles of accommodation and assimilation. Yet while their surface features coincide, their deeper or underlying structures diverge. On the surface level, for example, Piaget's notion of accommodation, or the passive adaptation to environmental inputs, is similar to my conception of experiential centeredness (or constraint), and his notion of assimilation, or the active transformation of environmental inputs, is comparable to my tenet of experiential fluidity (or expansion). At the level of their *existential* implications, however, the respective principles depart. Whereas Piaget's conceptions cleave to relatively overt (e.g., physiological and cognitive) developmental processes, my notions of centeredness and fluidity extend to the affective, intuitive, and symbolic. Hence, from my view, not only is centeredness associated with constraints of cognition or environment, but also with constraint (mortality, insignificance) before being. Likewise, fluidity is not merely connected with physiological or cognitive dexterity, but with the challenge of existentially standing out, venturing forth, and losing control. See K.J. Schneider, *The paradoxical self* (see above Chapter Two, note 6) for an elaboration of this developmental perspective.

Notes to Chapter Three

1.   Cited in W. Kaufmann, ed., *From Dostoyevsky to Sartre* (New York: New American Library, 1975), 77.

2.   H. Hesse, *Siddhartha* (New York: Bantam, 1951), 143.

3.   S. Freud, *Introduction to psychoanalysis* (New York: Pocket Books, 1924/1963), 80. See also M. Merleau-Ponty, *The phenomenology of perception* (London: Routledge Kegan Paul, 1962) on "ambiguity" in psychological perception.

4.   See H. Marcuse, *One-dimensional man: Studies in the ideology of advanced industrial society* (Boston: Beacon Press, 1964). The one-dimensionality of late-capitalist society has multiple sources, but patriarchy, Calvinism, and utilitarianism are among the leading strains.

5.   See R. May, *The meaning of anxiety* (New York: Norton, 1977) for an elaboration on the reductionism of anxiety and its cousin sensibilities, ambivalence and ambiguity, to physical warning mechanisms. While May recognizes the adaptive value of so-called signal anxiety, he argues with equal vehemence that such anxiety must be seen in a much larger light. Not only is anxiety a signal of impending physical danger, contends May, but it is also a signal of the struggle of life itself, the struggle, that is, between one's actuality and potentiality.

6.   See M. Berman, *The twilight of American culture* (see above Chapter Two, note 7) and M. Csikszentmihalyi, "If we are so rich, why aren't we happy?" *American Psychologist*, Vol. 54 (1999), 821–827.

7.   K. Zernike and M. Petersen, "School's backing of drugs comes under fire." *New York Times*, (8/19/01), pp. A–1 and A–29.

8.   Ortega y Gasset, *Revolt of the masses*, p. 65 (see above Chapter Two, note 36).

9.   For a lively exploration of multiple personal identities, see J. Rowan, *Subpersonalities: the people within us* (New York: Routledge, 1995) and F. Nietzsche, *Beyond good and evil* (New York: Vintage, 1966) on masks. Also of note is E. Mendelowitz's masterful *Ethics and Lao Tsu: Intimations of character* (manuscript submitted for publication, Boston, MA).

10.   For a classic disquisition on Feudal carnival psychology, see M. Bhaktin, *Rabelais and his world*, trans. by H. Iswolsky (Bloomington, IN: Indiana University Press, 1984).

11.   M. Bhaktin, *Rabelais and his world*.

12.   M. Bhaktin, *Rabelais and his world*. See also K. McLoughlin, *Shakespeare, Ra-*

belais, and the comical historical, unpublished manuscript, Marymount Manhattan College, 1999.

13.   O. Rank, *The double* (New York: New American Library, 1971).

14.   E. Becker, *Beyond alienation* (New York: Brazillier, 1967), 213.

15.   An updated version of this statement can be found in *Towards a global ethic: An initial declaration,* available from The Council for a Parliament of the World's Religions, 70 E. Lake, Suite 205, Chicago, IL 60618. The statement was initially drafted in collaboration with the renowned theologian, Hans Kung.

16.   Ironically, this secular thrust is becoming religious. Led by President George W. Bush and the neo-conservative movement, the United States (and capitalism in particular) is acquiring a kind of idolatrous status among a number of its constituents. But as Tillich had warned, the mistaking of a finite (that is, human) identity for that of an infinite (or godlike) identity can have grave consequences. As far back as 1963, Tillich cautioned:

> Even without the danger of extremist movements, there is a danger that the American…consciousness may slowly become, in combination with American power, a quasi-religious element for many people… .Now I do not think that direct fascism is the real danger. It is more a hidden replacement of the really ultimate [i.e., God] by the ultimacy of the so-called 'American way of life.' This term to me has questionable connotations because it fixes something. And it contradicts the 'new beginning' [i.e., open-minded] character of original American life. (Cited in *Ultimate Concern* [New York: Harper-Colophon, 1965, 68–69]).

See also K. Armstrong, *The battle for god* (New York: Ballantine, 2000) and B. Barber, *Jihad vs. McWorld* (see above Notes to Background, note 4) for support for this interpretation.

17.   As a result of "collateral damage," an estimated 13,000 Iraqi civilians were annihilated in the 1991 Gulf war, and over 6000 more have died since the most recent (March, 2003) U.S.-led attack which was launched ostensibly to eliminate Iraq's weapons of mass destruction (see the London-based website www.iraqibodycount.net). See also E. Epstein, "How many Iraqis died? We may never know," *San Francisco Chronicle*, May 3, 2003, A-13. As of this writing, however (February, 2004), neither weapons of mass destruction nor stability have resulted from these aggressive actions, and glaring questions remain about their credibility.

18.   See AFL-CIO, *Corporate compensation committee rigged to overpay CEO's* www.paywatch.org, April, 1999 and Southern Poverty Law Center, *Intelligence Re-*

port, Fall, Issue No. 96, (1999), 8. If current trends continue, the disparities in both income and living standards in our society are likely to grow much larger. For a provocative reflection on the social implications of a high debt, minimalist government economy, see J. Stiglitz, "The roaring nineties: A new history of the World's most prosperous decade" (New York: Norton, 2003).

19.   For compatible earlier visions see E. Fromm, *The sane society* (Greenwich, CT: Fawcett, 1955); E. Becker, *Beyond alienation* (New York: Brazillier, 1967); R.D. Laing, *The politics of experience* (New York: Ballantine, 1967); the majestic D. Whyte, *The heart aroused: Poetry and the preservation of the soul in corporate America* (New York: Doubleday, 1994); T. Pauchant, *In search of meaning: Managing for the health of our organizations, our communities, and the natural world* (San Francisco: Jossey-Bass, 1995); and M. Lerner, *The politics of meaning: Restoring hope and possibility in an age of cynicism* (Reading, MA: Addison-Wesley, 1996). See also B.P. Kennedy, I. Kawachi, D. Prothrow-Stith, K. Lochner, and V. Gupta "Social capital, income inequality, and violent firearm crime," *Social Science and Medicine*, Vol. 47 (1998), 7–17.

20.   See D. Bar-On, "First encounter between children of survivors and children of perpetrators of the holocaust," *Journal of Humanistic Psychology*, Vol. 33 (No. 4, 1993), 6–14. Also see M. Pilisuk, "Humanistic psychology and peace," in K.J. Schneider, J.F.T. Bugental, and J.F. Pierson, eds., *The handbook of humanistic psychology*, 115–126 (see above Notes to Introduction, note 2).

Notes to Chapter Four

1.   R. May, *Love and will* (New York: Norton, 1969). "The Great Conversation" is a quote from R. M. Hutchins, cited in E. Becker, *Beyond alienation*.

2.   See E. Becker, *Beyond alienation* (see above Chapter Three, note 14). This finding is consistent with similar findings that control, commitment, and challenge are integral to vocational well-being (see S. Kobasa, S. Maddi, and M. Pucecetti, "Type A and hardiness," *Journal of Behavioral Medicine*, Vol. 6 (1983), 41–51).

Notes to Chapter Five

1.   R. Otto, *The idea of the holy*, 6 (see above Notes to Introduction, note 1).

2.   Cited in H. Thomas, "Keeping person-centered education alive in academic settings," in K.J. Schneider, J.F.T. Bugental, and J.F. Pierson, eds., *The handbook of humanistic psychology*, 558 (see above Notes to Introduction, note 2). There is increasing evidence that the neglect of play in educational institutions—and particu-

larly at the pre- and primary school levels—is having a shocking effect on childhood brain development, social and emotional maturation, and ability to think. When we ask "what brings students alive?," then assuredly computerization and standardized testing are not our optimal answers. For an elucidating inquiry into these predicaments, see S. Olfman, ed., *All work and no play: How educational reforms are harming our preschoolers* (Westport, CT: Greenwood, 2003).

3.   E. Becker, *Beyond alienation* (see above Chapter Three, note 14).

4.   "Awe-based" education is not to be confused with President George W. Bush's notion of "faith-based" education. Although awe-based and faith-based perspectives can certainly converge, they are also likely to radically diverge. For example, whereas faith-based education appears to stress traditional religion, awe-based education is proposed to embrace the spiritual and philosophical underpinnings of traditional religion.

5.   Cited in R. May, *Paulus* (New York: Norton, 1987), 114.

6.   Theonomy, for Tillich, is the state of dynamic tension between autonomous (or human) reason and divine (or spiritual) law. This tension is also integral to awe; the awe-curriculum raises ever-deepening questions about both our estrangement from and connectedness to spirit (or being). See P. Tillich, *Systematic theology*, Vol. 1 (Chicago: University of Chicago Press, 1951), 85–87.

7.   Cited in E. Becker, *Beyond alienation*, 56 (see above Chapter Three, note 14).

8.   See R. May, *The cry for myth* (New York: Norton, 1991).

9.   W. Wachhorst, "Touching the sky: How science has lost its wonder…and what our schools can do about it." *San Francisco Magazine*, December (1999), 35–42.

10.   For an example of such facilitation, see M. O'Hara, "Emancipatory therapeutic practice for a new era: A work of retrieval," in K.J. Schneider, J.F.T. Bugental, and J.F. Pierson, eds., *The handbook of humanistic psychology*, 473–489 (see above Notes to Introduction, note 2).

11.   For an elaboration on how such a vision may actually be implemented by psychology, see K.J. Schneider, "Toward a science of the heart: Romanticism and the revival of psychology," *American Psychologist*, Vol. 53, No. 3, (1998), 277–289.

Notes to Chapter Six

1.   P. Tillich, *The courage to be* (New Haven, CT: Yale University Press, 1952).

2.   R. Otto, *The idea of the holy* (see above Notes to Introduction, note 1).

3.   P. Tillich, *The courage to be*, 62–63 (see above Chapter Six, note 1).

4.   P. Tillich, *The courage to be* (see above Chapter Six, note 1).

5.   R.M. Rilke, *Letters to a young poet* (New York: Norton, 1934/1993), 67.

6.   B. Pascal, *Penseés*, 1654, cited in M. Friedman, *The worlds of existentialism* (Atlantic Highlands, NJ: Humanities Press, 1991), 38.

7.   See F.X. Barron, *Creativity and psychological health* (New York: Van Nostrand, 1963); J.P. Guilford, *The nature of human intelligence* (New York: McGraw-Hill, 1968); and K.J. Schneider, *The paradoxical self* (see above Notes to Chapter Two, note 6).

8.   See C.G. Jung, *Two essays on analytical psychology*, trans. by R. Hull (Princeton, NJ: Princeton University Press, 1966). These essays originally appeared in 1928 and 1943, respectively. See also K.J. Schneider, *The paradoxical self* (see above Notes to Chapter Two, note 6).

9.   See P. Tillich, *The courage to be* (see above Chapter Six, note 1) and R. May, *Freedom and destiny* (New York: Norton, 1981) for an elaboration.

10.   See C.G. Jung, *Two essays on analytical psychology* (see above Chapter Six, note 8) and K.J. Schneider, *The paradoxical self* (see above Notes to Chapter Two, note 6).

11.   A. Camus, *The myth of Sisyphus and other essays*, trans. by J. O'Brien (New York: Knopf, 1955).

12.   V. Frankl, *Man's search for meaning: An introduction to logotherapy* (Boston: Beacon Press, 1959/1992).

13.   Cited in K. R. Jamison, *Touched by fire*, 119 (see above Chapter Two, note 24).

14.   See D.G. Hartwell, *Foundations of fear* (New York: Tom Doherty Associates, 1992), 1–11.

15.   K.J. Schneider, *Horror and the holy* (see above Chapter Two, note 16).

16.   See, for example, the articulate description of this sequence in J. Herman, *Trauma and recovery* (New York: Basic Books, 1997).

17.   See V. Frankl, *Man's search for meaning*, 139 (see above Chapter Six, note 12). See also P.T. Wong and P.S. Fry, eds., *The human quest for meaning: A handbook of psychological research and clinical applications* (Mahwah, NJ: Lawrence Erlbaum, 1998).

18.   S. A. Rubin, "The dynamism of resolute being: The experience of tragic optimism in an existential worldview—A heuristic investigation," Ph.D. dissertation,

Center for Humanistic Studies Graduate School, Detroit, MI, 2002. This dissertation is also important from the standpoint of the so-called "positive psychology"
movement, which has captivated mainstream professional psychology. Positive
psychology aims to "measure" the "good life," according to its chief spokesperson
and past president of the American Psychological Association, Martin Seligman. See
M. Seligman, "What is the good life?" [president's column], *American Psychological
Association Monitor,* October, 1998. But what it may not be able to "measure," nor
calibrate as "good," is the sublimity of human growth processes—the dark depths
as well as rosy surfaces. See S. Resnick, A. Warmoth, and I. Serlin, "The humanistic
psychology and positive psychology connection: Implications for psychotherapy,"
Journal of Humanistic Psychology, Vol. 41 (2000), 73–101.

19.   S. A. Rubin, "Response to debate over Dennet's "bright" article posted last
week," *Dialogues* Listserve, August 31, 2003 at louiselu@frontiernet.net.

Notes to Chapter Seven

1.   H. Ellenberger, *The discovery of the unconscious: The history and evolution of
dynamic psychiatry* (New York: Basic Books, 1970).

2.   For examples of experientially based depth psychotherapy, see R. May, *Discovery of being* (New York: Norton, 1983); J.F.T. Bugental, *The art of the psychotherapist*
(New York: Norton, 1987); and K.J. Schneider and R. May, *The psychology of existence* (see above Chapter Two, note 28).

3.   I elaborate on this case in great detail in my chapter, "Existential-humanistic
psychotherapies," in A.S. Gurman and S.B. Messer, eds., *Essential psychotherapies*
(New York: Guilford, 2003) 149–81.

4.   See G. Roth *When food is love* (New York: Plume, 1991), 183–184.

5.   See the Transhumanist website at www.aleph.se/Trans/index.html.

6.   On "intentionality" in psychotherapy, see R. May, *Love and will* (New York:
Norton, 1969).

Notes to Chapter Eight

1.   This chapter elaborates on my article "Enchanted agnosticism," *Tikkun* Vol. 18,
July/August, (2003), 41–43.

2.   See P. Tillich, *The courage to be* (see above Chapter Six, note 1).

3. E. Burke *A philosophical enquiry into the sublime and beautiful* (New York: Penguin, 1757/1998).

4. P. Tillich, *Dynamics of faith* (see above Chapter One, note 3).

5. P. Tillich, *My search for absolutes* (New York: Simon & Schuster, 1967), 130.

6. I. Berlin, *The roots of romanticism* (Princeton, NJ: Princeton University Press, 1999).

7. S. de Beauvoir, *The ethics of ambiguity,* trans. by B. Frechtman (New York: Citadel, 1962).

8. C. Gilligan, *In a different voice: Psychological theory and women's development* (Cambridge, MA: Harvard University Press, 1982).

9. E. Becker, "The heroics of everyday life: A theorist of death confronts his own end," interview with S. Keen, *Psychology Today*, April (1974), 78. Part of the quotation is from the audiotape of the interview, available from *Psychology Today*.

10. See M. Heidegger, *Being and time* (New York: Basic Books, 1962) and M. Nussbaum, *Upheavals of thought: The intelligence of emotions* (New York: Cambridge University Press, 2003).

11. B. Spinoza, *"On the improvement of the understanding;" "the ethics;" "correspondence,"* trans. by R.H.M. Elwes (New York: Dover, 1955), 260–271.

12. M. May and L. Olszewski, "No more excuses: Oakland school works to turn students into lifelong learners," *San Francisco Chronicle*, January 16, 2001, A-4.

13. M. May and L. Olszewski, "No more excuses" (see above Chapter Eight, note 12).

14. Since the advent of managed care, there has been a plethora of such stories, some associated with the most notorious crime sprees. See, for example, "Racist shootings test limits of mental health system, and laws," *New York Times*, August 14, 1999, A1 and A8.

15. E. Erikson, *Childhood and society* (New York: Norton, 1963).

16. J.F.T. Bugental, *Psychotherapy and process: The fundamentals of an existential-humanistic approach* (Reading, MA: Addison-Wesley, 1978).

17. J.F.T. Bugental, *Psychotherapy and process* (see above Chapter Eight, note 16).

18. The internally, relatively free can be compared favorably with the creative personality, according to recent studies. See, for example, chapter 3 in C. Csikszentmihalyi, *Creativity* (see above Chapter Two, note 29).

19. B. Woodward, "Chilling advice for hijackers," *San Francisco Chronicle*, September 28, 2001, A-1 and A-5.

20. Quoted in R. Knoll, *The Jung Cult: Origins of a charismatic movement* (New York: Free Press, 1994), 135.

21. Quoted in W. McGuire and R.F.C. Hull, *C.G. Jung speaking: Interviews and encounters* (Princeton, NJ: Princeton University Press, 1977), 194.

22. H.E. Barnes, *An existentialist ethics* (New York: Knopf, 1967).

23. This book actually owes something of a debt of gratitude to Heidegger, particularly the later Heidegger. His calls for a more poetic style of life and his trenchant critiques of technocracy are indeed resonant with much that I call for in the present volume. However, there is something seclusive about these calls to the aesthetic, something removed, which I have attempted to avoid. As Maurice Friedman has pointed out in *The worlds of existentialism* (Atlantic Highlands, NJ: Humanities Press, 1991), xvii-xix, Heidegger's aestheticism was vague, solipsistic, elite, and, during the Nazi period of course, ill-fated. Today we are challenged by a new aestheticism, and democratization is its key.

24. H. Ott, *Martin Heidegger: A political life* (New York: Basic Books, 1993).

25. Quoted in H.E. Barnes, *An existentialist ethics*, 420 (see above Chapter Eight, note 22).

26. H.E. Barnes, *An existentialist ethics*, 31 (see above Chapter Eight, note 22). and A. Camus, *The myth of Sisyphus and other essays* (New York: Vintage, 1955), 147–151.

27. For an elaboration on the implications of these heritages, see C.G. Jung, *Memories, dreams, and reflections*, edited by A. Jaffe (New York: Vintage, 1963); R. Safransky, *Martin Heidegger: Between good and evil* (Cambridge, MA: Harvard University Press, 1998); and R. Knoll, *The Jung cult: Origins of a Charismatic Movement.*" (New York: Free Press, 1994.)

28. J.A. Garraty and P. Gay, eds., *The Columbia history of the world* (New York: Harper & Row, 1972). See also W. Shirer, *The rise and fall of the third Reich: A history of Nazi Germany* (New York: Simon and Schuster, 1960).

29. Quoted in C. Carson, ed., *The autobiography of Martin Luther King, Jr.* (New York: Warner Books, 1998), 33.

30. M.K. Gandhi, *The way to God* (Berkeley, CA: Berkeley Hills Books, 1999), 51.

31. M.K. Gandhi, *The way to God*, 91 (see above Chapter Eight, note 30).

32. For an elaboration on these and related issues, see O. Rank, *Art and artist: Creative urge and personality development* (New York: Knopf, 1932); R. May, *Love and will* (see above Chapter Seven, note 6); R. Lifton, *The Nazi doctors: Medical killing and the psychology of genocide* (New York: Basic Books, 1986); T. Kirsch, *Jung and the Jungians: A comparative historical perspective* (London: Routledge, 2000); D. Bair, *Jung: A biography.* (Boston: Little, Brown, 2003); and M. Lila, *The reckless mind: Intellectuals in politics* (New York: New York Review of Books, 2001).

33. W. Whitman, *Leaves of grass*, edited by M. Cowley (New York: Penguin, 1855/ 1976), 145.

34. W. Whitman, *Leaves of grass* (New York: Modern Library, no date), 422.

35. P. Tillich, *Dynamics of faith*, 100 (see above Chapter One, note 3). Tillich's distinction between two forms of mysticism—that which embraces purity, fusion, and nonduality, and that which comprises ambiguity, paradox, and the dialectic—resides at the center of a crucial theological debate. This debate has been carried on for years by such writers as Pascal, Kierkegaard, and Nietzsche, but is now expressed through articles in such periodicals as *The Journal of Humanistic Psychology, The Humanistic Psychologist* (of the Division of Humanistic Psychology of the American Psychological Association), and *The Handbook of Humanistic Psychology*.

36. P. Tillich, *Dynamics of faith*, 57 (see above Chapter One, note 3).

37. E. Becker, "The heroics of everyday life" (see above Chapter Eight, note 9).

Notes to Chapter Nine

1. Perhaps the answer is a new "theology of nature." See M. Ruse, *Darwin and design: Does evolution have a purpose?* (Cambridge, MA: Harvard University Press, 2003), 335. A theology of nature is a theology that "appreciates the complex, adaptive glory of the living world, rejoices in it, and trembles before it" (335).

2. See for example, C. G. Jung, *Answer to Job*, trans. by R.F.C. Hull (New York: Bollingen Foundation, 1958).

3. See A. Wolfe, "The final freedom," *The New York Times Magazine*, March 18, 2001, 48–51.

4. For a fascinating discussion of our contemporary identity disorder, see E. Mendelowitz, "Fellini, Fred, and Ginger: Imagology and the postmodern world" in K.J. Schneider, J.F.T. Bugental, and J.F. Pierson, eds., *Handbook of humanistic psychology*, 153–159. See also his *Ethics and Lao Tsu: Intimations of character* (see above

Chapter Three, note 9).

5.   These potentialities are superbly investigated in E. Cardena, S.J. Lynn, and S. Krippner, eds., *Varieties of anomalous experience: Examining the scientific evidence* (Washington, DC: American Psychological Association, 2000).

6.   See K. Wegela, *How to be a help instead of a nuisance: A practical guide to giving support, service, and encouragement to others* (Boston: Shambala, 1996).

7.   E. Conze, *Buddhism: Its essence and development* (New York: Philosophical Library, 1951), 40.

8.   P. Tillich, *Systematic theology* (Chicago: University of Chicago Press, 1963), 231.

9.   P. Tillich, *My search for absolutes*, (New York: Simon and Schuster, 1967),109.

10.   P. Tillich, *My search for absolutes*, 109 (see above Chapter Nine, note 9).

11.   P. Tillich, *My search for absolutes*, 109 (see above Chapter Nine, note 9).

12.   P. Tillich, *My search for absolutes*, 110 (see above Chapter Nine, note 9).

13.   P. Tillich, *My search for absolutes*, 111 (see above Chapter Nine, note 9).

14.   R. J. Lifton, *The protean self: Human resilience in an age of fragmentation* (New York: Basic Books, 1993).

15.   M. Merleau-Ponty, *The phenomenology of perception* (London: Routledge and Kegan Paul, 1962), xx.

16.   See E. Hoffer, *The true believer* (New York: Harper and Row, 1951).

Notes to Chapter Ten

1.   For an elaboration on "enchantment," see chapter one of M. Berman, *Reenchantment of the world* (see above Notes to Background, note 2). On "agnosticism" see T.H. Huxley, *Agnosticism and Christianity* (Buffalo, NY: Prometheus Books, 1992). By "agnosticism" Huxley meant "insufficiency of evidence" or "suspension of disbelief." On this point see W.L. Reese, *Dictionary of philosophy and religion: Eastern and Western thought* (Atlantic Highlands, NJ: Humanities Press, 1980), 7. The radical behaviorist B.F. Skinner was an agnostic in this sense because he, too, refused to speculate upon non-measurable data, and he ignored such data at the experiential level. See B.F. Skinner, *Beyond freedom and dignity* (New York: Knopf, 1971). However, scientists do not universally share such sentiments. Indeed, some of

the greatest philosophers of science, such as Ludwig Wittgenstein and Alfred North Whitehead, imply that it is precisely where science (in the traditional sense) reaches its limit that life becomes most interesting. Again, see W.L. Reese, *Dictionary of philosophy and religion*, 622–625, 630–632.

Albert Einstein, despite his hardcore rationalism, divulged:

The most beautiful and most profound emotion we can experience is the sensation of the mystical. It is the sower of all true science. He to whom this emotion is a stranger, who can no longer wonder and stand rapt in awe, is as good as dead. To know that what is impenetrable to us really exists, manifesting itself as the highest wisdom and the most radiant beauty which our dull faculties can comprehend only in their most primitive forms—this knowledge, this feeling is at the center of true religiousness (cited in L. Barnett, with a foreword by A. Einstein, *The universe and Dr. Einstein* [New York: Bantam, 1957], 108).

2.   See K. Armstrong, *A history of god: The 4,000 year quest of Judaism, Christianity, and Islam* (New York: Ballantine, 1993), 205. See also E. Pagels, *Beyond belief: The secret gospel of Thomas* (New York: Random House, 2003).

3.   The kernel of this idea can be found in the enchanted yet agnostic writings of Emmanuel Levinas on "face to face" human encounter. See E. Levinas, *Totality and infinity* (see above Chapter Two, note 39). See also the dialogical meditations of Martin Buber and Maurice Friedman. For example, see M. Buber, *I and thou* (see above Chapter Two, note 39) and M. Friedman, *Religion and psychology: A dialogical approach* (New York: Paragon House, 1992). See further, A. Mindell, on *The deep democracy of open forums: How to transform communities* (Charlottesville, VA: Hampton Roads, 2002), as well as California State Senator John Vasconcellos' Web site—http://www.politicsoftrust.net.

4.   C. Rogers, "The rust workshop: A personal overview," *Journal of Humanistic Psychology*, Vol. 26 (1986), 23–45. See also M. Pilisuk, "Humanistic psychology and peace" in *The Handbook of Humanistic Psychology* (see above Introduction, Note 2) and M. Lerner, *Spirit matters* (see above Notes to Background, note 2).

5.   C. Rogers, "The rust workshop," 36 (see above Chapter Ten, note 4).

6.   C. Rogers, "The rust workshop," 39 (see above Chapter Ten, note 4).

7.   Cited in M. Berman, *The twilight of American culture* (New York: Norton, 2000) 9.

Index